the green kitchen

Richard Ehrlich

the green kitchen

techniques & recipes for

- cutting energy use
- saving money
- reducing waste

Kyle Cathie Ltd

For my daughters, Rebecca, Alice and Ruth

And for my nieces and nephews: Sam, Mickey and Margie Ehrlich; Hazel and Harry Wodehouse; Daniel and Jason Ehrlich; Anna, Emily and Tom Dally; and Matthew Hollingworth

First published in Great Britain in 2009 by
Kyle Cathie Limited, 122 Arlington Road, London NW1 7HP
www.kylecathie.com

ISBN 978-1-85626-804-2

*Pages with photography by Jason Lowe, home economy by Janie Suthering and styling by Penny Markham: 50, 52, 59, 93, 116, 119, 127, 147, 155, 165, 177, 183, 196, 202.

Editors Caroline Taggart and Jenny Wheatley
Designer Mark Jonathan Latter @ Pink Stripe Design
Home economy and styling Sarah Tildesley
Production director Sha Huxtable

A Cataloguing in Publication record for this title is available from the British Library.

Printed in Singapore by Tien Wah Press.

Printed on 100% recycled paper.

contents

Introduction   6

1 Equipping the Green Kitchen   8

Recipes and Cooking Techniques
2 Lidded Cooking   28
3 Microwave Cooking   64
4 Pressure Cookers   98
5 No-cook Cooking   138
6 Cooking for Multiple Meals   148

7 Greener Cleaning   186
8 Reducing Waste   198

Index   206
Useful Web Addresses   208
Acknowledgements   208

introduction

Since Lewis Thomas wrote the words quoted opposite some 35 years ago, his predicted revolution has occurred. And its implications have become far more urgent. Planet Earth faces a disaster brought about by the irresponsible carelessness of the human race. Every single one of us has to play a part in controlling the Earth's life responsibly, and this book suggests some ways of going about it: through small changes in everyday kitchen habits which can minimise their environmental impact.

Your kitchen consumes finite resources in numerous forms: the energy you use to prepare food and cook it; the water you use for cooking and washing; the 'embedded energy' in your foodstuffs, their packaging, and the equipment used for storing and cooking them. You also produce waste whenever you peel an onion or wash a dirty frying pan.

The expenditure of those resources and the creation of waste are inevitable. With very little thought, however, you can cut both those things in your own kitchen. That's what this book is about: cutting your personal contribution to the worldwide problem.

The Green Kitchen is partly a cookbook, with recipes based on the most energy-efficient cooking methods: using lidded pots and pans, the microwave oven and the pressure cooker. In addition to the recipes it also has extensive tips on environmentally friendly practice in the less glamorous areas of kitchen life: washing dishes, using appliances, waste reduction, kitchen cleaning and so on. It is not a book that sermonises. Nor does it make extravagant claims for the environmental benefits that arise when a single home cook does what I suggest. It is a book about making hundreds of small changes in everyday kitchen practice that will add up to large-scale benefits if adopted in thousands of households. In a sense, it is about becoming part of a large, informal community of Green Kitchenistas.

The practices I suggest are not onerous. Once you get used to them, they become part of your routine. They are no more difficult for kitchen neophytes than for 50-year veterans, and they won't cost you a penny. On the contrary, most of what I recommend here will save you money rather than costing you more. Energy prices have risen tremendously in recent years, and *The Green Kitchen* deals with numerous energy-saving ideas. You will also save money by using less water, if your water is metered, and you will save additional sums – sometimes quite large over the course of a year – by switching to greener cleaning methods.

Again, I am not suggesting that your solitary efforts will save the planet. This book is about the small changes that each of us can make. Imagine that you are one of thousands, or tens of thousands, all working together for the common good. If you think that way, you are never alone – even when it's just you in the kitchen, with the radio on.

The degree to which we are all involved in the control of the earth's life is just beginning to dawn on most of us, and it means yet another revolution for human thought.

LEWIS THOMAS, THE LIVES OF A CELL: NOTES OF A BIOLOGY WATCHER

1.
equipping the green kitchen

Every kitchen is stocked with hardware that falls into three categories: essential, optional and unnecessary. The Green Kitchen is stocked, ideally, with nothing from the third category and mostly items from the first. But every home cook will have his or her own categories for different items. One person's essential food processor is, for another person, an unnecessary bit of hardware that uses up space. The more space they take up, and the more energy they use to operate, the harder you have to look at them when deciding whether to buy. This chapter is designed to help with those decisions.

dishwasher

New dishwashers use far less of both energy and water than their older counterparts. On average, according to the Energy Saving Trust, new energy-efficient dishwashers use around 40 per cent less energy than those made in the technological Dark Ages known as the late twentieth century.

According to Waterwise, while pre-2000 machines use an average of 25 litres of water per load, newer machines use an average of just under 15 litres; some use as little as 10 litres. Calculating on Waterwise's average figures, running an old machine twice a week would use around 1,000 litres more per annum than a new machine.

But do you need a dishwasher in the first place? If you resist buying one because it uses more water and energy, you may well be mistaken. According to Waterwise, 'Hand-washing can be very efficient if you use a bowl and watch how much you use. But daily hand washing typically uses about 63 litres and if dishes are rinsed off under a running tap the total water used can be 150 litres.' These findings are borne out by research conducted at the University of Bonn by a group of volunteers, which found that the dishwasher used around half the energy and one sixth the water of hand-washing.

This research may not stand up if a hand-washer is exceptionally careful in the use of heated water. And the study did not account for the 'embedded energy' in manufacturing or recycling the machine.

If you choose not to buy a dishwasher for whatever reason, you must hand-wash dishes efficiently, minimising both water and energy use. Look at the tips on page 188 for advice.

Whatever fridge/freezer you buy, make sure it's at least A-rated for energy efficiency. The gradings, which are scrupulously enforced by government agencies, run from A+ to G. There's no excuse for buying anything less than A: it doesn't cost any more than the less efficient grades.

fridge/freezer

It's obvious that you need a fridge and a freezer, unless you're a teetotal vegan who never needs ice cubes and never stores fresh vegetables for more than a few days. Everyone else has to keep certain things cold, whether for health reasons (animal protein in any form, liquid or solid) or palatability reasons (white wine, salads, etc.). And unless you never use ice cubes, you need a freezer of some size.

But what fridge, and what freezer? That's something you have to decide on the basis of your needs – and if you buy more capacity than you need, you are wasting not just money but energy. Very large 'American-style' fridge-freezers can use over 500kWh per annum, around 75–100 per cent more than smaller appliances, and may have between 200 and 300 per cent more storage capacity.

The difference won't bankrupt you or contribute seriously to climate change; indeed, those large appliances can be considered more efficient in terms of energy consumption per cubic litre of storage space. But they're still the wrong choice if you don't need something so big. And if everyone bought an unnecessarily power-hungry fridge-freezer, electricity would be wasted on a grand scale.

some tips for efficient operation

- Check the temperature of the fridge, ideally by using an accurate stand-alone thermometer. It needs to maintain a maximum temperature of 5°C for food-safety reasons, and anything too far below that is a waste of electricity. Remember, too, that the fridge will need to be turned up (i.e. lower temperatures) in summer, and down in winter when the room is cooler.

- Defrost the fridge periodically. If there's an ice build-up, it will operate less efficiently.

- Don't overfill or crowd the fridge. It should be around 75 per cent full for maximum efficiency. If it's a modern-style fridge with a fan that circulates air, don't block the fan.

- Check the seal around the door to make sure it's shutting properly. A useful test: close the door with a thin sheet of paper (a banknote works well) sticking out. If the sheet falls or droops, the seal needs cleaning or possibly replacing.

- If you're defrosting something, put it in the fridge overnight. This is advisable for food-safety reasons, but it also provides 'free' cooling energy and cuts electricity consumption, because the fridge won't have to work as hard to keep the temperature down.

oven

With ovens as with refrigeration, look for ratings of energy efficiency on an A to G scale. Fan ovens are generally regarded as more fuel-efficient than ordinary ovens because they cook faster: if a recipe calls for cooking at 200°C/400°F/gas mark 6, for instance, you can set a fan oven to 180°C/350°F/gas mark 4 and it will cook at roughly the same speed. But the fan itself uses electricity, and some studies in the USA suggest that this can reduce the overall savings to the point where there is little difference between conventional and fan ovens.

Another point to consider: most ovens nowadays are electric. If you're using electricity generated by non-renewable fossil fuels, the electric oven is inherently less green than gas. According to one set of figures from the University of Sheffield, 1kWh of electricity releases 422g of CO_2 into the atmosphere while 1kWh of gas releases 194g. But the options are limited here, as there are so few gas ovens around. The greenest option is to buy your electricity from a completely green supplier.

Self-cleaning ovens are more energy-efficient than standard ovens because their thicker insulation (needed to withstand the high temperature used for cleaning) means they lose less heat to the surrounding air. If you can afford the considerable extra expense, you'll shave a bit off energy use and therefore running costs. But see the note opposite on using the self-cleaning function.

some tips for efficient operation

There's much more scope for cutting down energy consumption from an oven by the way you use the oven itself. Some of these tips are covered elsewhere, but a quick summary:

- Don't use the oven for foods that can be cooked using a different method.

- If you're roasting or baking in the oven, turn the oven off for the last ten minutes of cooking. Retained heat will continue cooking your food at exactly the same speed.

- Remember that preheating accounts for much of an oven's energy use. Don't use the oven if you're just cooking one dish that cooks quickly; always try to use it for cooking more than one dish at a time.

- Don't open the oven door repeatedly during cooking. Heat is lost and the oven has to switch back on again to replace it.

- If you have a self-cleaning oven (you lucky thing!), don't clean it too often: this is the most energy-gobbling of the oven's functions.

- Unless you use the oven constantly, you don't need to give it a full clean more than once every couple of months. Wipe it out in the meantime, and consider using a non-stick lining sheet on the base (see page 26). And when you do use the self-cleaning function, try to do it when the oven is already hot from cooking. The ideal scenario: bake some bread at the end of the day (bread needs a high heat), then switch to self-clean and let the oven work overnight.

- Get an oven thermometer. The one built into your oven may not be accurate, and the actual temperature may be much higher than the oven's settings indicate. If that's the case, you are using more energy than you need to – as well as running the risk of overcooked food.

- If you live alone, you may be able to do without a full-size oven and use a combination microwave oven or a free-standing 'mini-oven' instead. These preheat faster because of their size, and they have a lower output in watts. But the greatest savings come from using the microwave and convection oven together, because the microwave speeds up cooking. See page 20 for more detail.

hobs

Gas is cheaper than electricity, and produces fewer CO_2 emissions per kWh of energy produced. So, a gas hob is the best type to have, if you can get gas where you live. But it isn't that simple. Electric hobs deliver more of their heat energy to the cooking vessel than gas: upwards of 70 per cent, according to the United States Department of Energy, as compared with 35–40 per cent for gas. If this extra efficiency translates into faster cooking, the difference in energy use between gas and electricity narrows.

The most efficient electric hobs are (in increasing order of efficiency): radiant, halogen, induction.

Radiant hobs include the old-fashioned metal type with a spiral coil or a sealed plate, though some are now enclosed by ceramic or glass surfaces.

Halogen hobs use a powerful halogen lamp under a ceramic or glass surface to create bright red light and radiant heat; the heat energy starts warming the pot instantly, as fast as gas and with a more efficient transfer of energy.

Induction hobs work in a different way, creating an electromagnetic current which heats the pan directly. Induction hobs deliver 90 per cent of their energy to the pan, a higher percentage than any other hob type. They require no preheating, stay cool to the touch even when switched on, cool off instantly, and cook faster than any other hob – including gas. But they are also the most expensive type and can only be used with cookware that contains iron, so they're not for you if you like aluminium pots and pans.

some tips for efficient operation

If you get your electricity from a supplier that uses 100 per cent renewable energy, your carbon cooking footprint is lowest using electricity. But if that's not the case, gas, on balance, is the best option. And whichever hob you buy, some everyday practices will ensure that you use it as efficiently as possible.

- Use the right pan for the job, and on the appropriate ring. If the pan is too small, energy will be wasted heating the air (electric ring) or sides of the pan (gas).

- Replace warped pans if you have an electric hob. The more metal that's in contact with the ring, the faster it will heat and cook.

- If you use gas, don't turn it on until the pot is in place. And turn it off whenever it isn't in use, even if it's just for the few seconds needed to take one pot off a ring and put another one on.

- If you use an electric hob with old-style coils or metal plates, try using one ring to cook several dishes in succession rather than multiple rings to cook simultaneously. These hobs use a lot of energy to preheat.

- And, of course, cook using a pressure cooker or a lidded pan.

flooring

A kitchen floor has to look nice, wear well and be easy to clean. If you are thinking of getting a new kitchen, or just new flooring, you should be aware of the major alternatives and their cost to the environment. Evaluations of this kind are done using 'life-cycle assessment', which means putting together all the costs of manufacture, installation and disposal.

A study of this kind was done in 1997 on three major types of flooring: solid wood, linoleum and vinyl/PVC. The study, based on an assumed average lifetime of 40 years for wood, 25 years for linoleum and 20 years for PVC, found that wood flooring consumes the least energy in manufacturing, followed by linoleum and then PVC. It also found that over its life cycle, PVC had the potential to produce 2.5 times more greenhouse gases than linoleum and 10 times more than wood.

The message here is pretty clear: wood is the flooring of choice for the Green Kitchen. Ideally it should come from sustainably managed woodlands as close as possible to where you live, so that carbon emissions produced by transportation are minimised.

Prices vary widely, from low-end to very expensive, and specialist advice and installation are a must.

Bamboo, though a grass rather than wood, looks and behaves like wood in kitchen flooring. Grown in Asia, it doesn't meet the criterion of proximity to your home. But it is particularly hard-wearing and attractive, and it meets the sustainability criterion because it grows so rapidly – a matter of weeks rather than years. When shopping for bamboo, look for suppliers who use a minimum of formaldehyde in the adhesive. Prices are generally quite low.

Another ultra-green flooring material is cork, which by its nature is a sustainable product. Cork is harvested from mature trees which aren't damaged by the removal of their bark, and are ready to produce another crop within around 10 years. The tiles are usually at the lower end of the price scale, and come in a range of colours and patterns; you're not confined to the natural colour.

There is another alternative: rubber. The rubber must be 'natural' rubber, not a substitute made from a combination of rubber and PVC. Natural rubber is the sap of the trees, which are a renewable resource and an efficient CO_2 sink. The flooring can come in a wide range of colours and textures, and it's hard-wearing. But it's also expensive.

With all types of flooring, ease and frequency of cleaning is a major issue. The issue doesn't have anything to do with food safety, which in the Green Kitchen concerns food on preparation surfaces: these are the important danger areas. Dropped slices of cheese or salad leaves should be thrown away, unless you want to take a chance with micro-organisms lurking on what you think is a clean floor. The cleaning issue is aesthetic. A dirty floor doesn't look nice, and even those of us who aren't 'house-proud' don't like to see clear signs of grime when we look down. With all surfaces, this is easily dealt with by regular use of a

microfibre mop (see page 195), which will pick up dirt while employing no cleaning agent apart from water. If you insist on using stronger chemicals, you have to get detailed advice from the supplier of your flooring.

17

lighting

If you have a newish kitchen, I'll bet that it has recessed ceiling lights using halogen spotlights. And if that's the case, you have my sympathy. These bulbs need to be replaced often. And they waste a lot of money, producing needless CO_2 emissions in the process.

Low-voltage halogen bulbs are in effect spotlights, and act like a torch, just pushing light onto the floor, which is why so many are needed. Ordinary light bulbs produce 10 lumens (the standard measurement of light output) per watt. Low-voltage halogen bulbs produce 20 lumens, but that compares with a minimum of 60 lumens per watt for compact fluorescent bulbs. In some kitchens, low-voltage halogen might be gobbling up 1kW of energy where a couple of compact fluorescent bulbs could do the same job at 40 watts.

One solution is to have a combination of ceiling-mounted lamps for ambience and 'site-specific' lights for crucial work such as chopping vegetables. If you have bought recessed lights, you can switch over to compact fluorescents. While the best time to plan lighting is when you're designing a new kitchen, with good advice you can retro-fit.

The best choices for green lighting are compact fluorescent lamps (CFLs) and the even more energy-efficient light-emitting diodes (LEDs). CFLs are criticised by some for taking a minute or two to reach full brightness; but the newer bulbs light up faster. And even if they don't, it's easy to get used to the delay. Some people also think they emit a cold light; I've been using them all over the house for years, and this too is something you get used to. In any case, research is proceeding steadily towards production of CFLs that give a warmer light. With energy savings up 80 per cent using CFLs, most of us have no excuse for not using them. LEDs are still in their infancy with regard to domestic lighting systems. Here too, however, the research is making good progress. LEDs can now produce 100 lumens per watt, even more than CFLs, and when commercially viable they will be the technology of choice.

worktops

The choice of a worktop is one of the most important you can make when having a new kitchen put in: it affects the whole look and feel of the room. But the worktop has to be practical, too: waterproof, scratch-resistant, heat-resistant, and hard-wearing over a lifespan measured in decades. And it also needs to have as small an impact on the environment as possible.

The only clear-cut recommendation I can make is a top choice for worktops: wood from a sustainably managed source. Wood is carbon-negative while the tree is growing, acting as a sink for atmospheric CO_2. After the tree is felled, the energy used to process it is lower than the energy needed to manufacture any of the alternatives. If it comes from a local source, transport emissions are as low as they can be – unlike with granite, for instance, which may travel thousands or tens of thousands of miles. Sealing with non-toxic oil is the only treatment it needs after installation. And when the kitchen is eventually remodelled, the wood can be reused.

Countertops are a demanding area of the kitchen. They get a lot of use; they get wet and greasy and are subject to scuffing and scratching. It is a false economy to buy cheap, because you'll just have to replace them sooner – and that does the environment no favours, quite apart from the burden on your credit card. In buying, you have to try to balance the green credentials of each material against its cost and its quality. To take just one example: there are relatively inexpensive ceramic counter-tops that contain an element of recycled material, but they require a lot of energy in manufacturing and transport. There's always a trade-off, whatever you choose.

small appliances

Every time you buy a small appliance for your kitchen, your actions have an environmental impact in three different ways.

• The 'embedded energy' in the appliance itself – what was used to manufacture and ship it.

• The energy it will use in operation.

• The cost of disposal, whether through recycling or adding it to landfill.

This doesn't mean you shouldn't buy appliances! Some of them are useful, others would be viewed as essential by some home cooks. But if you're going to buy them, think first about what you want from them and whether they're really essential or just an occasional extra.

microwave oven

Since there's a whole chapter on microwave cooking in this book, you don't need to be told that I think they're great. But I will not hate you if you choose not to get one. Some people don't have space, and some people – misguidedly – just don't like the idea of them.

If you are thinking of buying a microwave oven, take comfort in the news that they've become steadily less expensive in recent years, so that basic models sometimes cost less than a good stainless steel saucepan. The oven should have a carousel on which the dish revolves so food cooks more evenly. It will have a range of power settings, plus (on nearly all models) some 'automatic' settings for things like defrosting, reheating, simmering and perhaps even cooking certain dishes. The 'automatic' settings may or may not be useful to you; I never use them myself.

The big decision in microwave buying is whether to buy a

combination oven – one that incorporates a grill and/or a convection oven. I owned one of these ovens at one time, and I sometimes used the extra features, but I cannot claim to be an expert on them. They are more expensive to buy, but in the long run they may save you money on energy bills. Why? There are two reasons.

One, they allow you to cook things faster in the microwave than you would in an ordinary convection oven. The combination of convection heating and microwave energy produces more energy than convection alone.

Two, the internal dimensions are smaller than those of a conventional oven, so they preheat faster. Indeed, you can probably do away with preheating altogether because the microwave energy starts cooking as soon as the oven is turned on.

On balance, if the extra expense poses no problems, I would advise getting a combination microwave in preference to an ordinary microwave. As you gain experience with it, the versatility may mean that you use your main oven less, and this should save energy. Indeed, some people don't have a conventional oven at all, using a combination microwave for all roasting and grilling.

blender

I personally regard a blender as an essential item, even though I don't use mine often. Buy a jug blender if you want to make fruity drinks or milky drinks, a stick blender if you'll be using it only for puréeing soups and cooked fruit. The best jug blenders have more powerful motors and therefore use more electricity – but they also work faster, so the difference in energy use is reduced.

The trade-off between stick and jug blenders is a tricky one. There is more embedded energy in a jug blender simply because it's bigger, and the motor is bigger so it uses more electricity per minute of operation; it also needs more water to wash. On the other hand, a jug blender works faster than a stick blender so the higher energy consumption of its motor may be offset by shorter blending times. Like so many green questions, this one has no perfect answer. I would say, however, that buying a more expensive but more robust jug blender is preferable to buying a cheap one. It will work faster and last longer.

kettle

Around 97 per cent of UK households have a kettle, and with the number of households rising, electricity consumption by kettles is set to rise too. This appliance can't get much more energy-efficient. So what can get more efficient? You and I.

But is a kettle the best way to boil water? I experimented by putting 500ml of water in a kettle, a 16cm milk pan (tightly covered) and a plastic measuring jug in the microwave. In the kettle, it took 1 minute, 37 seconds to boil. In the microwave, it took 4 minutes to reach 80°C. The milk-pan water, on a gas hob, reached a simmer at 5 minutes. Clear message: don't use the microwave. The kettle's heating element is much more efficient at transferring energy to the water.

The comparison with gas is more difficult; there are so many variables involved. But a similar experiment carried out by a consumer-oriented technology website found that CO_2 emissions using a gas hob were 15 per cent higher than those using a kettle. The figures for an electric hob were off the scale – though they would be much better on an ultra-efficient induction hob.

But kettles should be used with care, which means not over-filling. That's where you and I come in. According to the Energy Saving Trust, 'If everyone boiled only the water they needed... we could save enough electricity in a year to power the UK's street lights for seven months.'

key tips for energy-saving kettle use:
• If your kettle can't manage just a single cup's-worth of water, use the surplus to wash a wine glass or scrub the sink while the teabag is steeping.
• Do not put the kettle on and then leave the kitchen. You will forget about it. You will have to boil it again.
• Use your drinking cup to measure out the water you need.
• Do not buy a kettle that uses power when not in use, for an indicator light on base or jug. If you already have one, leave it unplugged.

what not to buy

juicers

The typical juicer uses somewhere between 400 and 1,000 watts of electricity. If you take a machine running on 1,000 watts, and use it for 5 minutes every day of the year, that's around 30kWh a year – which is roughly equivalent to one tenth the usage of a standard-size fridge-freezer. The juicer also needs to be cleaned after every use. You can get better nutrition from eating fruit and vegetables. Do you really need that juicer?

food processor

I own a food processor, and I almost never use it. I use it mainly for making shortcrust pastry, and that's just because I'm lazy about cutting the butter into the flour using knives. But I really don't need it, if truth be told.

Do you need one? This is a deeply personal decision. If you don't have one, and you have been cooking happily without it for a long time, you can probably live without one forever.

If you do have one, think about what you use it for. For chopping, grating or slicing large quantities of food, especially stuff like carrots and onions, it can be invaluable. For instance, the mass-produced soffrito on page 167 is one case where the food processor is unquestionably worth dusting off. Preparing that quantity of raw material would take ages by hand. But if you are using it for small tasks that could just as easily be carried out with a knife, you are wasting both electricity and the resources needed to wash the bowl and attachments. Not necessary.

And whatever you do, don't wash the jug in the dishwasher: it takes up too much space. The chopping disk is a different matter because it is so small, but the jug definitely calls for manual labour.

pots and pans

For serious cooking, every authority on earth will tell you that high-quality cookware is the only type to buy. And the authorities are correct. The quality costs you a lot more than cheap cookware, but it will serve you better in the kitchen – and for far longer.

Length of service is also the green argument in favour of buying the best. With the exception of enamelled cast iron, anodised aluminium, and PTFE-coated non-stick pans, well treated cookware of high quality will literally last

you for your whole life – and then be in good enough condition to pass on to your heirs! I know of families where the heirs of the deceased fought not about the jewellery or the bank account but about the cast-iron frying pan that Grandma always used to make her corn bread or tarte tatin. That's just the way it should be: nothing is greener than reuse. Of the three exceptions mentioned above, enamelled cast iron and anodised aluminium are nearly as long-lasting as stainless steel and uncoated cast iron. They need more care in use to promote longevity: avoiding very high heat, abrasive cleaning and metal utensils are the three key points. I have owned the same enamelled cast iron casseroles and anodised aluminium sauté pan for over 20 years. They perform as well today as they did when I bought them.

Non-stick linings do eventually wear away and the pans need replacing. And note also the reservations about PTFE on page 26. There is, however, a newer type of non-stick cookware (Green Pan) using a lining made just of sand and water. It eliminates the environmental concerns and is exceptionally hard-wearing.

food storage

Almost every bit of food I store in fridge or freezer gets stored in a plastic box. Those I use are Stack-a-Boxes, sold by Lakeland.

Stack-a-Boxes have long been performing most of the functions that clingfilm carries out in non-green kitchens. Whichever brand you buy, get a range of sizes, typically ranging from 400ml to 2.5 litres. Buy square boxes, which are more space-efficient than the yogurt pots and other round tubs that Green Kitcheners are likely to save for future use. (Go on saving them, by the way: they are useful things.) And buy boxes with tight-fitting clip-on lids.

There are alternatives to Stack-A-Boxes, one of which is even better. The Lock 'n' Lock range comprises sturdy polypropylene storage vessels with clips that snap the lid tight onto a silicone sealing ring. The seal is awesome. They never leak, even when shaken violently.

using plastic boxes

Use them for everything that you might otherwise store in squares of clingfilm or aluminium foil:

• Scraps of onion, ginger, chilli etc. Refrigerated, they can keep well for a week or even longer. You can use the same box over and over again unless it gets dirty or smelly.

• Leftovers. There is simply no need to wrap meat in film or foil, and cooked vegetables can be stored in either the fridge or freezer, for easy thawing and microwaving.

• Picnics. You can pack an entire meal for al fresco eating into a collection of boxes and your food will be compact, leak-proof and generally tidy.

non-stick baking sheets

This is a difficult subject to write about because the best sheets are those coated with PTFE (polytetrafluoroethylene), and PTFE has been proved fairly conclusively to entail health risks. The risks take two forms.

One is in manufacture, which uses a compound called PFOA (polyfluorooctanoic acid) which has been named as a 'likely carcinogen' by the US government. Until an alternative is found for PFOA, it is untenable to recommend buying PTFE products – and that applies to non-stick cookware as well.

The second risk, which I regard as minimal, lies in the kitchen: heating PTFE to high temperatures can release toxic gases. Now, the temperature needed to release the gases is very high – around 260–280°C. Ovens and empty frying pans do not usually get that high. If you are willing to read up on the subject in detail, and then to take a balanced view of the risk, you may want to continue using PTFE not just in cookware but in these baking sheets, which really are wonderful things.

There is an alternative: non-stick silicone sheets, the next best thing. They can't be cut to size, as PTFE sheets can, and they are thicker and therefore less flexible. But they too eliminate a lot of heavy-duty washing up. If you put them in a roasting pan or baking dish, you end up with a mucky sheet which is hand-washable or dishwasher-cleanable. And you don't have to scrub baked-on residues from a metal or ceramic dish – one of the most labour- and resources-intensive kitchen cleaning jobs.

what not to buy

aluminium foil

Certain kitchen jobs can only be carried out by aluminium foil. If you're baking something and need to seal it tightly, the heat-proof qualities and flexibility of foil are usually required. But not necessarily. Try using a PTFE or silicone sheet (see opposite) with a stiff baking tray on top.

Many of the other uses of aluminium foil can be duplicated by other things. For food storage, use plastic boxes instead. If you need to wrap something tightly for storage in the fridge or freezer, such as pastry or meat, use a clean carrier bag that can no longer be used for shopping.

And if you do use aluminium foil, make sure you recycle it: manufacturing aluminium is an energy-hungry process, and recycling cuts around 90 per cent of the cost in energy and raw materials. Clean the foil as thoroughly as possible before putting it in your recycling bin.

clingfilm

I have had the same roll of clingfilm for around 4 years, and I have used almost none of it. If I can do that, you can do it too. Clingfilm is made from petroleum products, and by not using it you are cutting use of fossil fuels and a small but long-lasting contribution to landfill.

The only time I miss clingfilm is when I'm cooking in the microwave: it is the most efficient means of sealing a microwaveable dish. But a plate makes a perfectly acceptable seal. Apart from that, I am living proof that clingfilm is simply unnecessary – and if you give it up, you won't miss it.

2.lidded cooking

When you cook something in a frying pan, saucepan or stockpot, the heat makes steam rise from the food and whatever liquid you are cooking with it. That steam is a form of energy, and it will escape if there's no lid on top. Sometimes this is necessary: you can't stir-fry with the lid on; and I don't like to simmer stock with a lid on for fear that the liquid will boil too hard and make the stock cloudy.

But numerous dishes that we cook in an open pan can be cooked with the lid on. This way you can cut the cooking time and energy use by as much as 75 per cent. Even if the cooking time isn't shortened, using the lid means you can cook at a lower heat, reducing your use of fossil fuels.

Some cookery writers and home cooks will protest that lidded cooking isn't suitable for certain foods. They claim that meat, for instance, won't get seared if there is steam around it, and some vegetables aren't suitable for cooking in a covered pot.

They are wrong. And you will discover this the first time you cook chicken or a chop with the lid on. Direct contact between the high heat of the pan's surface suffices to brown anything, while the parts of the food not in contact with the pan are cooking through by way of oil-bearing steam. With some meats, you won't even need to turn the pieces: by the time the downward-facing side is cooked, the top will be cooked too. With other foods, turning halfway through cooking works better. But either way, the results are as good as, and sometimes better than, the conventional open-pan methods.

Lid-use often results in another form of carbon-reduction. With some of the meat and poultry dishes here, lidded cooking replaces the grill or the oven – and both of these use more energy than cooking in a frying pan. In my method for pork chops (page 43), for instance, the effect achieved is comparable to that of grilling, which would take around 10 minutes of cooking plus preheating time. In the frying pan it takes just 2 minutes of energy use.

A final gain, though more one of convenience, is that you don't need to clean the hob of the splattered fat that inevitably arises during ordinary sautéing. You do get an oily lid, but this can usually be cleaned in the dishwasher (see page 194 for dishwasher use in the Green Kitchen).

Residual heat is just one more reason to adopt lidded cooking. Once you get used to this method, I guarantee that you'll use it more and more frequently. And your consumption of energy – not to mention your expenditure of time – will drop greatly.

residual heat

Another environmental – and culinary – advantage of lidded cooking lies in its exploitation of residual heat: the heat that stays in the pan and its contents even after the heat source is switched off. In some dishes, it can be used to complete the cooking without the use of external energy. This not only cuts down on energy use, in some dishes it also lets the meat 'rest' after cooking; resting distributes heat evenly throughout the dish and results in greater tenderness and juiciness.

lidded boiling

This is the no-skill, no-brain area of lid-use. Once the water in a pot has started heating to the point where it produces the first wisps of steam, you should pop the lid on. You can put the lid on from the beginning, of course, but it only starts to make a real difference once the water's already hot. On the other hand, putting the lid on straightaway does no harm – and it's a good way of remembering to use the lid if the practice is a new one in your newly Green Kitchen. The water will boil a little faster this way – and when you think of how many times you boil water in a year, the savings can amount to hours of energy use.

I am by no means the first person to observe that water boils faster when you keep the lid on. What's not so often noted is that you can also cook with the lid on, regardless of what you're boiling.

The cooking time might differ little from cooking times in an unlidded pot, but because you're trapping that steam energy inside the pot, you can apply less heat from below. In other words, you can use a lower heat – and thus much less energy.

My general rule of thumb on this:
• If you need to cook at a vigorous rolling boil, use a medium-low heat rather than full blast
• If you need to cook at a gentle boil, use a low heat rather than medium
• If you need to simmer, use the hob at its very lowest setting

There's just one bit of expertise you'll need to acquire with lidded boiling, and that is the ability to judge when the water's simmering or boiling at the correct rate. When you can't see the liquid, you need to use your ears – or just use a glass lid if you want to be able to see better. Once you've had a boiling-over incident (or two), you'll quickly get the hang of it.

The energy savings from lidded boiling are considerable. When I do it, I usually set the hob at around something between 10 and 25 per cent of its normal power for that kind of cooking.

But sometimes I don't keep the heat on at all. You can cook pasta by stirring it in the boiling water in the usual way, then putting the lid on and bringing it back to the boil. At that point, turn the heat off and cook the pasta for the time indicated on the packet.

Here is an example of lidded energy saving. I cook pasta at least once a week. Assuming a cooking time of 10 minutes, then that's at least 9 hours of heavily reduced energy consumption over a year. If you think about things that take more time to cook than pasta, such as pulses, you can see how many hours of energy-saving the lid can contribute.

One thing I don't simmer with a lid on top is stock containing fish, chicken or meat. I am a stickler for perfectly clear stock, and even the gentlest heat runs the risk of

cooking the stock too hard, resulting in some cloudiness. If you don't mind cloudy stock, by all means use a lid. Just keep an eye on it to maintain the heat at a very gentle simmer and not a boil. But since you'll be using a very gentle heat even if you cook stock without the lid, the energy saving is minimal using a lid. And the risk that the pot will boil over, or the stock go cloudy, if you leave it unattended leads me to stick to my unlidded guns. Just this once.

lidded boiling is suitable for:
Pasta
Pulses
Vegetables
Poached meat and poultry

lidded frying

Lidded frying is suitable for meat, fish and vegetables, though it's in meat and vegetables that you'll notice the greatest reduction in cooking times and/or energy use. This is simply because fish doesn't take much time to cook in the first place, at least in a frying pan. Having said that, I should add that you can slice a minute or two from the cooking time for any commonly fried fish, such as salmon steaks and fillets, or a piece of white fish.

a word on hardware

Chances are that you already own all the equipment you need for lidded frying. That is, a frying pan with a tight-fitting lid. The pan must be thick and heavy – preferably non-stick, though this isn't essential. A thin pan cooks too fast, and isn't good at preventing sticking unless you use prodigious quantities of oil.

If you don't own such a pan, I urge you to go and buy one. They are expensive, but with good care they will last for years – or forever, in the case of uncoated pans. Even the best non-stick pan will eventually lose some of its coating, especially if you use the high heat specified in some of these recipes. But this takes years if the pan is a good one.

I use the method most often, however, for poultry and red meat. It may seem counter-intuitive to cooks who have been taught to believe that the skin on a chicken leg won't crisp up and a steak or chop won't brown if they cook with steam present. Neither belief is based in fact. The chicken may need an extra minute or so with the lid off at the end of cooking to attain perfect crispness, but most of the cooking can be with that lid in place. Even without the lid-less phase, I promise that you and your fellow eaters will have no complaints. As for red meat: I've cooked it this way on hundreds of occasions, and no one – we're talking about some very discriminating diners here – has uttered a single objection. Can you please try it my way, just once?

fish

lidded fish en papillote

This dish saves resources in several ways. It takes 10 minutes of heat, rather than the 30 or so it would need in the oven (where dishes en papillote are usually cooked). The baking parchment can be composted, and the frying pan barely gets dirty as much of the cooking residues are trapped in the paper. But these green credentials are not the reason to cook it. The real reasons are that it tastes great and can be cooked quickly.

Serves 1 (to do more, simply multiply)

1 chunk (fillet or steak) of fish, around 2.5cm thick and weighing 200–250g
4 sprigs of dill
2 thin slices of lime
a generous knob of butter
salt and freshly ground pepper
1 tablespoon dry white wine

Cut off a piece of baking parchment measuring around 30 x 45cm. Put the fish at the centre, skin side down if the skin is still there. Put on the dill, then the lime and finally the butter. Season it with salt and pepper and pour on the wine.

Now fold up the paper to make a 'tent' for the fish. This is simple enough to do, though hard to describe. I find it easiest to bring together the two long sides of the paper and make a fold along their full length, then seal it tight with clean paper clips. Do the same at both ends.

Take an uncoated frying pan large enough to hold the parcel comfortably and heat it to medium-high. Put the parcel in and clamp the lid on. Cook for 5 minutes, then turn off the heat and leave for another 5 minutes so that residual heat completes the cooking.

To serve, place the parcel on the serving plate and let each diner unwrap his or her own to get a billow of fragrant steam. The paper clips should be left at the side of the plate and reused, rather than eaten.

salmon steak au poivre

This is a three-minute dish if you like rare salmon. If you like the fish to be fully cooked, it's a four-minute dish. If you want a low-cal meal cooked in a single pan (minimal washing-up), combine it with Lid-Steamed Celery (page 49) and it's a 10- or 15-minute meal. Cook the celery first, dump it into a serving bowl, and cook the fish. This method is for one steak, but it can served for a group as long as you use a large enough frying pan.

1 salmon steak, around 2.5cm thick
freshly ground black pepper
vegetable oil

Wipe one side of the salmon dry with a strip of paper towel. Pour oil into a heavy frying pan, preferably non-stick, to coat the bottom lightly; put the pan over a high heat. Set your peppermill to produce a coarse grind, and grind pepper onto the salmon to make a uniform coating that covers every bit of flesh. If you like a lot of pepper, grind on enough to hide the pink flesh completely.

Put the salmon in the pan with the peppered side down, season the top of the fish lightly with salt, and clamp the lid on. Set the timer for 2 minutes and turn the heat off when the timer goes off. Place the lid slightly ajar and leave the fish for 1 minute if you like rare salmon, 2 minutes if you like it fully cooked. Serve with the peppered side – which will have an attractively blackened look – facing up.

A lemon wedge completes the picture, though some chopped fresh herbs will add a bit of greenery and extra flavour.

poultry

chicken pieces under the lid

This is perhaps my basic lidded recipe, just because it's the one I cook most often. I call it 'roast chicken in a frying pan' (RCFP), even though it never gets anywhere near the oven. Unlike roast chicken, RCFP cooks quickly – little more than 15 minutes. It can be made for one, two, or perhaps a maximum of four people unless you are using two frying pans. And it requires just two ingredients: high-quality chicken pieces and some vegetable oil.

Lightly film the bottom of the pan with oil and put in the chicken, skin side down. Season with pepper and a tiny bit of salt. Put the pan over a high heat, cover it and wait till you hear the chicken sizzling vigorously. Turn the heat down to medium-high. Set a timer for 10 minutes.

When the timer goes off, turn the pieces, cover and cook for another 5 minutes. They may take another 5 after that, 10 at most; breasts could take longer than legs because they're thicker.

The result should be crisp skin and succulent, juicy flesh. If you want the skin crisper still, turn the heat down when the chicken's done and turn the pieces again so the skin gets a final blast of dry heat.

If you want to get really fancy, you can take the cooked pieces out and make a little gravy by deglazing the pan with wine/stock, a little flour (optional) and seasonings. But even without the gravy, you will have a delicious main dish.

red-cooked chicken

This Cantonese staple is just chicken poached with soy sauce (which gives the chicken its 'red' colour) and assorted flavourings. The Chinese themselves use lidded cooking here, so I am hardly the first person to discover the trick. To make it with a whole chicken, use a large saucepan or casserole which can hold the bird comfortably. And note: the amount of water needed will depend on the size of the pan and the number of pieces you're cooking. Use a pan of suitable size so you don't waste water: a 28cm pan will hold 4 breasts or 8 pieces of leg (thigh or drumstick); a single piece can be cooked in a 20cm pan, but use half the quantity of soy sauce.

Serves 4

2 garlic cloves, peeled and sliced
2–3 segments from a star anise
1 tablespoon brown sugar or honey
2–3 hefty slices of fresh ginger, peeled
200ml soy sauce, preferably dark
100ml Chinese rice wine or dry sherry
4–8 chicken pieces
around 1 teaspoon sesame oil per chicken piece

Choose a frying pan or sauté pan that will hold the chicken comfortably in a single layer; you don't need to worry about whether the pieces are crowded in the pan. Put all the flavourings and liquids in, then the chicken. Add enough water to nearly cover the chicken pieces. Cover, bring to the boil, then turn down to low and simmer, with the lid on, for 20 minutes (if the pieces are from a small bird) or 25 minutes if the bird was big. While the chicken is cooking, spoon cooking liquid over it a few times. Turn off the heat and leave with the lid on for 30 minutes.

Put a piece of chicken on each serving plate. Spoon and rub sesame oil over each piece, and eat with boiled rice. The leftover cooking liquid is very good for poaching vegetables in and can be added, in moderation, to other braised meat or poultry dishes.

feathered game

pheasant with bacon, port and grapes

Game birds pose a challenge for anyone who (like me) hates eating overcooked meat or poultry. They're naturally lean and therefore toughen easily if exposed too long to the heat. It's much better, in my view, when cooked *à point* like chicken – just to the point of doneness, with tender and juicy flesh. Lidded frying is a perfect solution: the flesh cooks gradually from steaming, while the skin can take on a bit of colour. The best birds for this method are pheasant, which should be cut in half (with the backbone removed) and partridge, which can be cut in half or (more impressive) left whole. Wood pigeon can also be cooked whole or halved.

Serves 2

2 thick rashers of streaky
  bacon, cut into thin shreds
  (lardons)
a little vegetable oil
1 pheasant, cut in half and
  backbone removed
salt and freshly ground
  black pepper
100ml ordinary port
  or dry red wine
12 red grapes
chopped parsley and a lemon
  wedge, to serve

Put the bacon in a pan with the vegetable oil and cook, uncovered, until it is lightly browned and has released a lot of its fat. Remove with a slotted spoon and set aside. There should be enough fat and oil to cover the bottom of the pan; add more oil if needed. Season the pheasant halves with a little salt and a lot of black pepper.

Put them in the pan, skin side down, and get them sizzling, then clamp the lid on and adjust the heat to maintain a steady sizzle. Cook until the skin is lightly brown, around 10–15 minutes, then turn the halves and continue cooking until the pheasant is just done, around 5–10 minutes more: the underside should be lightly browned and the breast meat should feel very firm when poked with your thumb. Remove to heated serving plates.

Put the bacon back in the pan with the port and grapes and turn the heat up to high. Let the liquid bubble away until reduced by just over half. Pour over the pheasant with the grapes and bacon, sprinkle with parsley, and serve with the lemon wedges. Rice or mashed potatoes make good side dishes here.

meat

beef steaks

These are in one sense among the easiest items to cook using lidded frying. The absence of a bone makes them lie perfectly flat, and they take well to the high heat. But beef is more time-sensitive than pork and lamb: some like it rare, some medium-rare, and so on – and if you like rare steak or medium-rare steak, even 30 seconds too much or too little can spell the difference between delight and despair. For this reason, giving timings for steak is exceedingly difficult. You will have to find your own way through experimentation. As a rough guideline, however, use these timings for any cut of steak around 2.5cm thick:

Rare	1 minute per side, with 2 minutes resting (heat off, lid on)
Medium-rare	2 minutes first side, 1 minute second side, with 2 minutes resting (heat off, lid on)
Medium	2 minutes both sides, with 2 minutes resting (heat off, lid on)

lamb loin chops

Choose a thick non-stick frying pan just large enough to hold the chops at least 2.5cm apart; if they're too close together, steam will rise in the spaces between them. The timings here are based on loin chops around 4cm thick. Put the pan over a medium heat with a little oil and, while it's heating up, place the chops in it with the fatty side lying on the pan's surface. This helps crisp up the fat and also makes it run a little, producing fat for frying. When the pan is hot, lay the chops flat to cook on the first side, clamp the lid on and set a timer for 2 minutes. When the timer goes off, turn the chops and cook for another minute. Now turn the heat off and leave them for another 1–2 minutes, depending on whether you like them pink or well done.

hamburgers

Hamburgers can be fried or grilled; both methods give excellent results, and I'm not opposed to them, but lidded frying simply speeds the process along and results in a burger that's every bit as good as a conventionally cooked burger. The timings here are based on a burger around 4cm thick, which I consider ideal. If you use a thinner disc of meat, make sure you cook the burger for a shorter time after flipping it. And since it won't be well browned on the second side, serve with the first side up. The accompaniments are up to you but I like some fried onions and perhaps a bit of greenery. Plus ketchup, of course.

Choose a thick non-stick frying pan just large enough to hold the burgers at least 2.5cm apart; if they're too close together, steam will rise in the spaces between them. Put the pan over a medium heat and, while it's heating up, cook some onions in it first, following the instructions on page 44.

When the onions are cooked, scrape them into a small bowl and wipe out the pan quickly with a piece of paper towel to remove any stray bits of onion. Add a little more oil to the pan, turn the heat up high, and put in the burgers. Clamp the lid on and cook for 3 minutes, then flip them and cook for another 1–3 minutes, depending on how you like them done. One minute will give you a rare burger, 2 medium-rare, and 3 medium.

lidded sausages

A rummage round the Green Kitchen cookery library, followed by some clicking round the web, has yielded a general consensus on the cooking of sausages. Frying: 10–20 minutes, very slowly, with regular turning. Grilling: 10–15 minutes, regular turning. Roasting (very good method): 20–40 minutes at 180–190°C/350–375°F/gas mark 4–5, turning once.

Discussion concluded? Not in the Green Kitchen. As usual, no one has mentioned the magic lid. When you cook sausages under cover, you cut the energy-consuming portion of the cooking time to a measly 3 minutes.

The challenge of cooking sausages is twofold. One challenge lies in their cylindrical shape: the tube never touches a flat cooking surface along anything more than around 45° of its 360° circumference. If the sausage has a comma-like curve, the curved surfaces never touch the pan at all. This is one good reason to grill or roast, where contact with a flat surface isn't necessary.

The second challenge lies in the need for heat control: it has to be hot or prolonged enough to brown the sausages deeply, but not so hot as to blacken the skins before the insides are thoroughly cooked.

The lid meets both these challenges. Generously film a stout frying pan, preferably non-stick, with vegetable oil. Put in the sausages, leaving a bit of space between them. Lid on, heat up high, wait for noisy sizzling. Turn the heat down slightly and set a timer for 2 minutes.

When the timer goes off, turn the sausages (watch for spluttering fat) and replace the lid. Set the timer for 2 minutes. When the timer goes off, turn the heat off and leave the sausages for 3–5 more minutes. Residual heat will ensure that they're cooked through, but not overcooked.

lamb fillet

By lamb fillet I mean neck fillet, a profoundly juicy, flavourful cut. This comes from the section of neck immediately adjoining the neck-end ribs which are sold as cutlets or rack of lamb. Neck fillet is sold by good butchers, who will cut it specially if you ask.

> Put the pan on a low-medium heat and film with vegetable oil. Put in the meat, pop the lid on, and cook for 5 minutes. Turn and cook for another 5 minutes. Turn the heat off and let the meat rest for 5–8 minutes.

pork loin chops

These work beautifully in a lidded frying pan, using the same timings as those for lamb chops on page 39. Except for one thing: you can't get the rind to turn to crackling. This isn't easy even under the grill, so there's no difference there. With the pan, however, you can produce great crackling as long as you're willing to do a little minor surgery on the chop and turn the heat on under the pan for a few minutes more.

> Cut the rind off the chop with as much of its underlying fat as possible. Cut the rind into pieces around 2.5cm long and put them in a pan, fat side down. Turn the heat on low and cover the pan. Let them sizzle gently for 3–4 minutes, then check them and press the pieces of ring down flat onto the pan surface. This aims to maximise contact with the pan and squeeze out melting fat. Continue cooking for around 5 minutes more, until they are crisp and crackled. Leave the lid off for the final 1–2 minutes of cooking, so any remaining water in the rind can cook out.
>
> Remove the crackled rind to a paper towel. Put the chops in the pan and fry them, with the lid on, over a high heat, for 3 minutes. Turn the chops and cook for another minute, then turn the heat off and leave them for another 3 minutes. They should be medium-rare, which is perfect for pork.

accompaniments

You can see from these recipes that I approach lidded frying as an ultra-simple method, with few if any additional ingredients going into the pan. This is intentional. First of all, if you get really good meat (and there's no point in buying any other kind), you don't need much to go with it. Let the meat speak for itself.

But for variety's sake, you will sometimes want (as I do) a little bit of extra flavour. When this is the case, you can do two things: cook something in the pan while it's heating up, or make a simple relish without using heat. Here are a few of my favourite things, suitable for use with any lid-fried meat or poultry.

fried onions

For each serving, cut a few thick slices of onion. Put them in a pan with a little vegetable oil and turn the heat up high, tossing the slices to coat with oil and seasoning with a little salt and pepper if you wish. When the onions start sizzling, turn the heat down to medium and stir-fry until they're lightly coloured and still very al dente. If you like, you can add some fresh herbs, finely chopped, towards the end of cooking. If you want the onions softer, pour in a good splash of wine or stock and let it cook away.

salsa verde

This is one of the world-champion sauces, so good you might be tempted
to eat it straight from the spoon. If you don't feel like doing that, serve it with
any plainly cooked meat, fish or poultry dish. Or with simply cooked potatoes
– it's a killer on mash. It's quite an oily salsa, so is perfect for lean meats
and vegetables cooked without oil. It's always worth making more than you
need because salsa verde keeps well in the fridge for a day or two, and
it's such versatile stuff.

Serves 8

2 large handfuls of flat-leaf
   parsley, finely chopped
3–4 tablespoons capers,
   finely chopped
1 tin of anchovy fillets, well
   drained and finely chopped
2 tablespoons red wine vinegar
around 150ml extra virgin
   olive oil

Mix all the ingredients and leave for at least 1 hour
before serving.

quick tomato, garlic and chilli relish

Serves 2–4

3–4 garlic cloves, finely chopped
1–2 small chillies, deseeded if you wish, and finely chopped
1 teaspoon whole cumin seeds
2 teaspoons vegetable oil
2 teaspoons red wine vinegar
2 ripe tomatoes, deseeded and coarsely chopped

Put the garlic, chillies, cumin and oil in a pan. Turn the heat on low and cook just until the garlic starts to sizzle. Add the vinegar and keep stirring until the vinegar is nearly cooked away. Add the tomatoes and cook, with regular stirring, until heated through and barely softened (around 2–4 minutes).

yogurt and dill relish

This is good with just about anything, but especially with pressure-cooked potatoes or green vegetables.

Serves 2–4

2 shallots, finely chopped
a large handful of fresh dill, coarsely chopped
a squeeze of lemon juice
1–2 teaspoons Dijon mustard
fine salt and freshly ground black pepper
around 200ml Greek or Bio yogurt

Put the shallots and dill in a bowl with the lemon juice and mustard, and stir well with a little salt and a generous grinding of black pepper. Now add 100ml of yogurt and stir well. Taste to see if there's enough yogurt, and just keep adding more until it has the intensity and consistency you want.

sour cream sauce

This comes from an old friend, Jeff Fields. It is delicious with chicken and fish.

Serves 4

200ml sour cream
100ml plain yogurt
juice of 2 limes
a large handful of fresh
   coriander, roughly chopped
1–2 green chillies, deseeded
   if you wish, finely chopped
1 green pepper
salt and freshly ground
   black pepper

Mix all the ingredients except the green pepper and refrigerate until needed. Just before you're ready to serve, deseed and chop the green pepper fairly finely. Mix in, season with salt and pepper and serve at once.

double-dipping sauce

This pairing of complementary sauces is designed for Hainan Chicken Rice in the late Yan-Kit So's *Classic Food of China*. It serves well with any mild-flavoured rice dish, congee (see page 133), or with roast chicken or pork.

singaporean chilli sauce

Serves 2–4

4 long chillies,
   deseeded and
   finely chopped
2 garlic cloves,
   finely chopped
2 tablespoons
   Chinese rice vinegar
1 teaspoon salt
1 teaspoon sugar

Combine all the ingredients and leave until needed.

cantonese ginger sauce

Serves 2–4

1 tablespoon grated
   fresh ginger
½ teaspoon salt
1 tablespoon
   vegetable or
   peanut oil

Combine all the ingredients and leave until needed.

vegetables

Lidded frying is one of the best methods for cooking vegetables that I know of.

The high heat of the oil gets a little colour into the vegetables, which translates as browning flavours with their extra dimension of complexity. There may also be a bit of crunchy texture from the browning. The method is like a cross between steaming and stir-frying, and it works well with a number of vegetables. The below is a sample recipe for lidded frying. It can be adapted for various green vegetables, carrots, or cauliflower cut into smallish florets, and many others besides. A crucial point: successful lidded frying depends on having the right quantity of vegetables in relation to the size of the pan. The pieces don't have to brown uniformly, but they mustn't lie in so thick a layer that the uppermost pieces get only steam heat.

lid-fried green beans

Serves 4 as a side dish

450g green beans
vegetable oil
salt
a few slices of red onion or
    3–4 spring onions, sliced
1 tablespoon soy sauce
1 teaspoon sesame oil

Top and tail the beans, and rinse them over a clean bowl. (Use the rinsing water for something else; it may even be clean enough for steaming or boiling or cooking in the pressure cooker.)

Put the beans in a heavy frying pan with a splash of oil and a little salt. Clamp on the lid and shake the pan to disperse the oil. Turn the heat on to high and, when it starts sizzling, set the timer for 1 minute. Toss the beans when the timer goes off and cook for another minute. Toss again. Do this until the beans are lightly browned and cooked al dente – around 4–5 minutes. When the beans are barely cooked, put the sliced onions on top and pour on the soy sauce and sesame oil. Toss well and serve hot or at room temperature. If you notice a very slight resemblance here to the classic Chinese dry-fried beans, you are very perceptive.

lidded steaming

For some vegetables, frying is either difficult or undesirable. These take better to steaming, which cooks them through without browning.

The recipe below, using celery, is a sample of the approach. Other good vegetables to use include peas, mangetout, broccoli and spinach. With lid-steamed vegetables as with fried vegetables, quantities are important. If the pieces are piled very high in the pan, those on the bottom will cook much faster than those on top. You can even out the cooking by tossing the contents of the pan halfway through cooking, but it will still be hard to get perfectly even cooking. If you're looking at a pan with layers more than three pieces deep, get out a larger pan!

lid-steamed celery

Serves 2

5–8 sticks of celery, trimmed and sliced 2.5cm thick
salt and freshly ground black pepper
½ teaspoon fennel seeds
extra virgin olive oil

Put the celery in a large, heavy pan which will accommodate them in a layer no more than around 4cm deep. Sprinkle on a little salt and pepper and add enough water to come around 1.5cm up the sides of the pan. Clamp the lid on, bring to the boil, then cook on a moderate heat for 3 minutes.

At this point, the vegetables should be cooked al dente – possibly very al dente. If you like them that way, go ahead and eat. If you like them softer, turn the heat off and put the lid back on. Residual heat will continue cooking the veg, turning them from al dente to soft (around 5 minutes) and then very soft (around 10 minutes). If there's water still left in the pan, remove the vegetables with a slotted spoon – or pour out the water, if you're being really green by serving the vegetables from the cooking pan. A quick toss with the fennel seeds and a little extra virgin olive oil is all the celery needs to be ready for eating.

lidded quick-braising

quick-braised lettuce

You will need a deep pan or heavy casserole with a high lid for this, as the lettuce is too thick to fit under the lid of an ordinary frying pan. A heavy casserole will do just as well. If you have the equipment, the results are an eye-opener.

Serves 3–4

1 Cos lettuce
chicken stock or water
a good knob of butter
red wine vinegar or lemon juice

Cut a lot of the end off the lettuce, as it is likely to harbour most of the dirt and grit. Loosely open out the leaves while trying to keep the lettuce intact, and rinse it over a bowl to clean thoroughly. It doesn't need to be dried.

Re-form the lettuce into something as close as possible to its original shape, then tie it securely with a long piece of string. Put it in the pan with enough chicken stock or water to make a shallow puddle – remember that there's already some water clinging to it from washing.

Clamp the lid on and cook on a medium heat for 10–15 minutes, with regular turning. The lettuce should be somewhere between al dente and soft. To serve, put on a serving platter and remove the string or loop. Cut into 4–6 pieces along the length of the lettuce, and drizzle on a little red wine vinegar or lemon juice.

the serial meal

If you hate washing dishes (and who doesn't?), you should try cooking a whole meal in the same frying pan. If you choose the right recipes, and cook them all with the lid on the pan to speed up cooking, you can have dinner cooked in 20 minutes. Here is a specimen meal of quick-braised celery, new potatoes, and sautéed pork chops.

Cook the celery first, over high heat in a little water or stock plus garlic for flavouring; cooking time, around 5 minutes. Put the celery into a serving bowl and replace it with small new potatoes, a bit of oil and a cup of water. Lid on, high heat, 7–10 minutes. Check the water after 5 minutes and add more if the pan is going dry. When cooked, put them in the bowl with the celery.

Now quickly rinse the hot pan, and put in the chops with a little bit of oil. Heat up very high. Lid on. Fry the chops violently for 2 minutes, then turn and cook for 1 (thin chops) or 2 (thick) minutes more. Turn the hob off and let residual heat finish the cooking. Reheat the vegetables in the microwave, if you wish. That's around 20 minutes from start-time to table-time. And there's just a single pan to wash up.

the hard-working lid

If you start getting into the lidded swing of things, you will have a battery of lids that need cleaning. Or don't need cleaning. To be precise: a lid that's been used to cook lamb chops or burgers will be coated with droplets (or worse) of the relevant fat, and will not be much good for anything else. They need to be washed, and the most efficient way of doing it is in a dishwasher. Wipe off excess grease with a dirty paper towel (see page 196) and put it in the machine in a way that ensures the water will have free access, i.e. not 'nesting' against a plate or some other large disc-shaped object, and not sitting on top of other washables.

If the lid has covered vegetables cooked with no or little oil or fat, consider whether it really needs to be washed at all. If no fat has hit it, it is not 'dirty' in any way that will affect the flavour or microbial safety of the next dish over which it sits. A quick wipe, especially with a wet Microfibre cloth (see page 195) will often suffice. Sometimes it doesn't even need that. As always in the Green Kitchen: think before you wash.

a few lidded favourites

Once you've got into the swing of lidded cooking, you will come up with your own variations on the essential principle. Here are just a few of mine.

courgettes and tomatoes

This is a true dish of summer, which is the time when both the main ingredients are at their best and most inexpensive. If you want, you can use halved cherry tomatoes instead of large tomatoes. For an Asian flavour, use vegetable oil instead of olive, 1–2 cloves of garlic and some finely chopped ginger.

Serves 4 as a side dish

extra virgin olive oil
2 large courgettes,
  thickly sliced
1 large ripe tomato,
  thinly sliced

salt and freshly ground
  black pepper
2–3 paper-thin slices of onion
around 2 teaspoons red
  wine vinegar
a small handful of fresh
  basil leaves

Place a pan over a medium heat. Pour in enough oil to make a shallow puddle, then put in the courgettes, followed by the tomatoes as a layer on top, and then the onion as a final layer. Season with salt and pepper.

Clamp the lid on and cook for around 5 minutes, until the courgettes are cooked al dente. Leaving them in there off the heat for 5 minutes with the lid on will make them fully soft, if that's what you want. Dress with vinegar and top with torn basil leaves.

cabbage with caraway

Caraway is a perfect match with cabbage, as is amply recognised in the cooking of eastern Europe. But the basic idea is so good, and the main ingredient so versatile and inexpensive, that I've put in a few variations.

Serves 4 as a side dish

white cabbage
a generous knob of butter
½ teaspoon caraway seeds
fresh dill, to finish

Core the cabbage, cut it in half lengthwise, and slice it around 1.5cm thick. Put the butter in a thick, heavy frying pan and melt it gently; there should be enough to coat the bottom of the pan generously. Add more if necessary. Put in the cabbage, toss thoroughly in the butter, then put in the caraway seeds and toss again.

Add a small splash of water, just enough to moisten the bottom of the pan, and cover. Cook over a medium heat for around 15 minutes to get cabbage that's soft but with a hint of bite, or for longer if you want it to be perfectly soft. Stir once or twice during cooking if the cabbage is in a thick layer in the pan.

variations

• Use whole Asian spices, especially cumin and coriander seeds, instead of dill and caraway.

• Use plain vegetable oil with a garlic clove and a small knob of fresh ginger, and season at the end with ½ teaspoon sesame oil and 1–2 chopped spring onions.

• Use duck or goose fat instead of butter.

• Quickly and lightly brown some fairly thin shreds of good bacon in the pan before cooking, then toss the cabbage in the melted fat and cook everything together.

quickest lid-braised cabbage

This is a quicker and simpler cabbage dish, best made with the pale inner leaves of a Savoy cabbage.

Serves 4 as a side dish

1 small Savoy cabbage, cored, cut in half lengthwise and into 1cm thick slices
2 tablespoons vegetable oil or duck fat
salt and freshly ground black pepper
around 150ml good chicken or beef stock

Put the cabbage in a frying pan with the oil or fat and a good dose of salt and pepper. Toss thoroughly to coat the leaves as much as possible with the oil or fat, then add 100ml of stock and clamp the lid on. Bring to a sizzle and turn the heat down to medium.

Cook for 5 minutes, stirring once, and checking the liquid while you stir; if it is cooking away, add a little more. After 5 minutes the cabbage will be done al dente. Leaving it covered with the heat turned off will soften it further.

lidded asparagus

Standard methods for cooking asparagus use a fair bit of energy – and a lot of water, if you're following the classic French method. The method here produces perfect, tender spears – with almost no energy and little water. Needless to say, it should be made only when asparagus is in season.

Serves 2–4 as a side dish

450g asparagus spears, trimmed
salt

Lay all the spears flat in a large frying pan with just enough water to cover the bottom. Apply a little salt and put the lid on. Bring the pan to an energetic boil, then let it cook for 1–2 minutes, depending on the thickness of the spears.

Now turn the heat off and keep the lid on. Set a timer for 3 minutes and test. If they aren't done, cover and leave for another few minutes.

stuffed mushrooms

Baked mushrooms are a fine thing, but they need at least 20 minutes of cooking in the energy-hungry oven. This alternative needs as little as 4 minutes of cooking, without the need for preheating. It's a quick dinner, if you plonk it down on a mound of buttered noodles and sprinkle on Parmesan. It's a quick lunch, if you use a piece of toast instead of the noodles. And it's an elegant dinner-party starter, if you cook one per person and just serve it on its own with shavings of Parmesan. Versatile, huh? The quantities are for one serving, and flavourings can be varied endlessly.

Serves 1

1 large, open or
   portobello mushroom
8–10 sprigs of parsley,
   finely chopped
1 small section of lemon zest,
   finely chopped
a few diminutive drops of
   balsamic vinegar
around 1 tablespoon extra virgin
   olive oil
1 small garlic clove or 1 shallot,
   finely chopped
salt and freshly ground
   black pepper

Break or cut out the remaining stem from the mushroom. Chop it finely and mix with the parsley, lemon zest and balsamic vinegar. Heat a tiny bit of oil in a heavy non-stick pan and cook the garlic or shallot just long enough to make it smell fragrant (around 1 minute).

Toss with the parsley mixture, then with around 2 teaspoons of the oil. Season with salt and pepper and spoon the mixture into the mushroom cap.

Put a little more oil in the pan and add the stuffed mushroom. Clamp the lid on and cook over a medium heat until the mushroom is lightly browned underneath and well softened throughout, around 5–10 minutes. You can also turn off the heat after around 3 minutes and complete the cooking with residual heat. If there are any mushroomy juices in the pan, pour them over the mushroom once it's on the plate.

creamed celery with red peppers

This little dish of celery and peppers is rich, soothing and deeply flavourful. Vegetarians could serve it on pasta or rice, with plenty of Parmesan. Omnivores could treat it as a side dish for fish or chicken. And note: adding 600ml or so of rich chicken stock would turn this into a sumptuous soup.

**Serves 4 as a side dish,
  2 as a main course**

1 head of celery, washed and
  thickly sliced at an angle
1 garlic clove, finely chopped
a very large knob of butter
1 teaspoon mild curry powder
salt and freshly ground
  black pepper
2 red peppers, deseeded
  and thinly sliced
60ml strong chicken or
  vegetable stock
50ml double cream
1 bunch of spring onions,
  trimmed and cut into pieces
  around 2.5cm long

Put the celery, garlic, butter and curry powder, if using, into a large frying pan. Add a generous dose of salt and black pepper and put over a low heat.

Cover the pan and cook very gently for 5 minutes, giving the contents a stir every minute or so, just to soften the celery a little. Add the peppers and mix well, then add the stock and cover. Cook this way for 10–15 minutes, stirring occasionally, until the vegetables are done the way you like them. Now add the cream and spring onions and cook for a few more minutes until the liquid is thick and gooey. The dish can easily sit for half an hour if reheated just before serving.

Carrots are good when raw, but truly
memorable when cooked in a flavourful
liquid. This recipe gives the flexibility to
cook them with lots of crunch or at full
melting softness.

glazed carrots with honey

This is adapted with great simplification from *My Gastronomy*, by the
great chef Nico Ladenis (written in close collaboration with the late Alan
Crompton-Batt). You can make as many of the carrots as you like, as long
as they all fit in the pan in a single layer – and they're very good for
keeping in the fridge for several days. The ideal liquid is homemade
chicken stock; second choice is five parts water to one part dry white
wine; third choice is plain water. Don't use a stock cube for this one.

medium-sized carrots,
   quartered lengthwise and cut
   into 5cm pieces
½ teaspoon runny honey per
   whole carrot
salt and freshly ground
   black pepper
butter
liquid (see above)

Put the carrots in a frying pan just large enough to hold
them. To give you an idea: a 24cm pan will hold
300–400g of carrots prepared in this way. Spoon the
honey on top, season with salt and pepper, and dot
with butter, as generously or lightly as you and your
doctor see fit. Now pour in just enough liquid to coat
the bottom of the pan.

Put over a high heat, clamp the lid on, and cook for
3 minutes once the heat has reached a mighty sizzle.
Check once in this time to make sure the liquid isn't
cooking away, and add more if it is. After 3 minutes the
carrots should be done al dente. Leaving them off the
heat with the lid on will turn them progressively softer.
After 10 minutes, they should be very soft.

potatoes

potatoes for mashing

Many cooks cling to a cherished, mythical belief that if you slice potatoes before boiling them to make mashed potatoes, they will absorb water and make watery mash. I have tested the myth over many years, and know that it isn't true. For perfectly done spuds, ready to mash, proceed as follows.

Peel the spuds and slice to the thickness of a £1 coin. Put them in a saucepan with plenty of water, bring to the boil, then turn the heat down and simmer for 5 minutes with the lid on. Turn off the heat, and finish cooking through residual heat for 5–10 minutes more.

'roast' potatoes in a pan

A lidded pan produces something exceedingly delicious in around a quarter of the time needed for real roast spuds. And the method requires little oil, so there's a calorie advantage too. The potatoes must be small ones, no more than around 5cm at their thickest point.

Generously film the bottom of a heavy frying pan with vegetable oil. Cut the potatoes in half along their longer axis: this exposes more flesh and makes them lie flatter in the pan. Put them in the pan, cut sides down, and make sure that the cut surfaces are well coated with oil. Add a little water – just enough to fill the pan to a depth of around 1cm.

Put the lid on and place the pan over a high heat. When the oily water starts to boil, turn the heat down to medium and set the timer for 10 minutes. Check them when the timer goes off by poking a small, sharp knife into the centre of a few pieces. There should be just a little resistance, and the water should have cooked off. Cook for 5–6 minutes more on a slightly lower heat, then check one or two pieces to ensure that the bottoms are well browned. If they are, the spuds should be just about done. Test again with the knife. When they're perfectly soft, they are done. But you can also turn the pieces to get a little colour into a bit of the skin. Drain on paper towels before serving with a sprinkling of salt.

lidded new potatoes

I think lidded frying is the best way to cook new potatoes. The skins get a little colour, with a secondary gain in the form of browning flavours, and the oil crisps them up slightly. The only thing you need to watch for is fitting frying pan to potato supply: the spuds must be in a single layer so they all get direct pan heat. This means that doing the dish for more than 4–5 people may be difficult unless you use more than one pan.

Generously film the bottom of a heavy frying pan with vegetable oil. Add the potatoes, in a single layer, then enough water to fill the pan to the depth of your little fingernail. Put the lid on and turn the heat up high. When it starts to sizzle, turn it down slightly and cook for around 10 minutes. Shake every few minutes to promote browning all over; the potatoes won't be uniformly brown, but that doesn't matter.

When the potatoes are just about done, turn the heat down to low and wait for it to drop; you can tell by the quieter sizzling. Add some chopped onion or garlic and some rosemary and cook for another couple of minutes, till the potatoes are tender. Save a few minutes of energy by turning off the heat and leaving residual heat to do the rest.

a few lidded pasta sauces

The lid speeds things up on a mid-week evening when you want to eat soon. Here are three sample approaches, all endlessly variable. They will sauce around 500g of pasta, enough for three or four people.

sausage and tomatoes

vegetable oil
4 sausages, cut into chunks
   (use scissors)
300ml dry white wine
20–25 cherry tomatoes
3 small garlic cloves, finely
   chopped
6 large button mushrooms,
   thickly sliced
a small pinch of dried
   herbs – oregano, rosemary
   or mixed herbs

Put a heavy, non-stick pan over a medium heat and pour in enough oil to film the bottom generously. Add the sausages. Once they've started sizzling, turn them quickly and clamp on the lid. Cook for 2 minutes, stirring and scraping once to detach any sausage pieces that are sticking to the pan.

Pour in the wine, and stir and scrape the sausages again. Add all the remaining ingredients and put the lid back on. Cook for another minute, then turn the heat off and leave for at least 1 minute more. If not serving immediately, leave to sit with the lid open so the steam doesn't cook the tomatoes too much longer. Left this way, the sauce can happily sit for 10 minutes or more. Reheat if necessary and add the cooked pasta to the pan so you save yourself the trouble, water and energy needed to wash a serving bowl.

peppers and basil

Great for vegetarians. If you can get long, thin peppers, their excellent flavour and firm flesh will make this simple dish even better. You can use just one colour if that suits you but a combination adds to the aesthetic appeal.

around 150ml extra virgin
   olive oil
4 peppers, preferably a
   combination of red and
   yellow, deseeded and cut into
   thick shreds
salt and freshly ground
   black pepper
100ml dry white wine
1 small red chilli, deseeded
   if you wish, and finely chopped
2–3 garlic cloves, thinly sliced
a large handful of fresh
   basil leaves, roughly torn
grated Parmesan, to serve

Put a heavy non-stick pan over a medium heat and pour in enough oil to film the bottom generously. Add the peppers, season with salt and pepper and stir well to coat the peppers with oil. Pour in the wine and clamp the lid on. Cook, stirring once or twice, until the wine has cooked down and the peppers are soft enough to eat but still retaining a good hint of bite. Put in the chilli and garlic, and cook for another 1–2 minutes – or longer, over a lower heat, if you want to diffuse the intensity of the full garlic flavour.

Left this way with the lid on and off the heat, the sauce can happily sit for 10 minutes or more. Reheat if necessary, and add the cooked pasta to the pan so you save yourself the trouble, water and energy needed to wash a serving bowl. Add enough extra virgin olive oil to make the sauce easy to toss, and top with the basil. This dish likes lots of grated Parmesan.

maccheroncini alla saffi

This recipe is based on one in Marcella Hazan's *Second Italian Cookbook*, and it's appropriate to use the original Italian name. Hazan got it, in turn, from a restaurant in Bazzano (Emilia-Romagna) called Ristorante della Rocca. The original called for prosciutto; Hazan uses boiled ham. I have reverted to prosciutto, which is barely cooked because it doesn't need cooking. Apologies to all concerned. And in case you're wondering: the dish is named after Aurelio Saffi, a governor of the Republic of Rome in the nineteenth century.

500g asparagus spears, trimmed
   and cut into 2.5cm lengths
a good knob of butter
150ml double cream
100g prosciutto, torn into
   thin shreds
grated Parmesan
finely chopped fresh parsley,
   to serve (optional)

Lay all the asparagus pieces flat in a large frying pan with just enough water to cover the bottom. Put the lid on, bring the pan to an energetic boil, then let it cook for 3–4 minutes; check halfway through to make sure the water isn't boiling away, and add a little more if it is.

When the asparagus is cooked – soft, but with a good hint of bite – pour out any remaining water and add the butter and cream. Simmer for a minute or so, just long enough to heat the cream through. Now put in the prosciutto, give everything a good stir and pour over the cooked pasta. Grated Parmesan completes the picture, though you could also sprinkle on some finely chopped parsley if you wish.

3.
microwave cooking

Microwave ovens are ubiquitous but neglected. Most people use them solely for secondary processes – defrosting, reheating and heating up of convenience foods – rather than for primary cooking. This is a terrible waste.

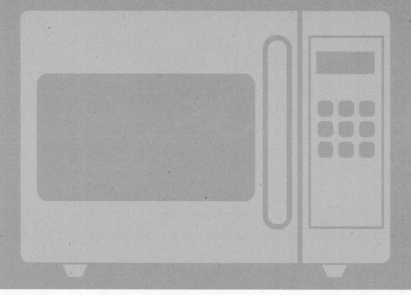

If you decide to start treating your microwave with respect, I urge you to buy Barbara Kafka's *Microwave Gourmet* – by far the best book on the subject and one of the most distinguished cookbooks ever published.

The microwave is not just an exceptionally useful cooking tool but exceptionally energy-saving. It cooks a number of dishes in less time than they'd take using a conventional cooking process and also, often cooks in what can then be used as the serving dish – so you're saving on washing as well as time. And this means saving natural resources, both energy and water.

If you already use a microwave oven, please bear with me while I explain the basic principles to newcomers.

• Microwave ovens cook food by sending out pulses of energy that cause water and other molecules to change position billions of times a second. That rapid movement creates heat, which cooks the food.

• The pulses penetrate the food only to a depth of around 2.5cm. Heat is conducted from the outer areas to inner areas, as it is when cooking food in a conventional oven, but microwave ovens are unsuitable for very large pieces of meat.

• If you are cooking something much thicker or deeper than 5cm, you need to turn it or stir it regularly during cooking. Things get a bit more complicated if you have a combination oven (see page 20).

Once you've mastered the basics, microwaving is as satisfying as any other form of cooking. The view of microwave ovens as a mindless tool is simply inaccurate: they require just as much skill, attention and care as any other cooking method.

At the same time, they have a tremendous advantage over hob-based cooking which is admirably summed up by my wife: 'The great thing about the microwave is that you put it on for 2 minutes and then it stops. You don't have to worry about answering the phone and forgetting that a pot is on the hob, boiling away.'

When you consider the savings in energy (and time) over other methods, you'll want to use the simple recipes and methods here for your own experimentation.

cooking vessels

There is no question that foods cook faster in plastic than in glass or ceramic. To get a benchmark, I heated 200ml cold tap water in a plastic measuring jug for 2 minutes. At the end, it was 93°C. When I heated the same amount of equally cold water for the same time in a ceramic coffee mug, it recorded a temperature of 80°C.

Does this mean you ought to buy plastic cookware for use in your microwave? Well, maybe. You can buy dishes of many types designed specially for use in the microwave, and I've used a few of them. In my view, they are not necessary: the dishes you already have will probably suffice for most uses. Just two words of caution:

• Ceramic dishes must be used with care, as they sometimes contain metal in the glaze which will overheat and may crack the dish – or at the very least get super-hot so it's dangerous to handle without oven gloves or something similar. Any crack in the dish is also likely to be worsened, as it may harbour a trace of water which will expand on heating.

• Plastic dishes must also be used with care. Unless a dish is specified as being microwave-safe, try it out by putting it in your microwave along with a jug containing some water. Heat at full power for a couple of minutes, then touch the dish to see if it's hot. If it is, don't use it in the microwave. This test is suggested in the excellent book *What Einstein Told His Cook*, by Robert L. Wolke. It can also be used, by the way, for ceramic dishes.

a note on timings

With microwave cookery, as with the pressure cooker, giving precise and infallible timings is extremely difficult. This is true of any cooking method, by the way. It just means that you have to pay attention to what you're doing and treat the timings as a guide rather than a rule.

That kind of caution is even more important with the microwave because you're deprived of two of your most useful cooking senses: smell and sound. The need for smell is an obvious one: you can tell by the smell whether garlic is burning, steak is getting charred, and so on. The sense of sound is no less important, though it's rarely mentioned by cookery writers. It can tell you, for instance, whether the liquid has boiled away in a steamer; whether a casserole is bubbling too hard; whether a super-hot roasting tin is shooting off jets of the fatty pan juices onto the walls and ceiling of your oven.

You can hear some of the sounds coming from the microwave if they're loud enough – sizzling fat, for example, makes a loud popping sound. But you can't smell anything at all. That's why, in every bit of microwave cooking I do, I always proceed gradually –

and I urge you to do the same. In the recipes here, I suggest testing and usually stirring the food every minute or two. That's probably excessive, but please try doing things that way to start with.

If you do the same, you will achieve two things, both of them good. One: you are highly unlikely to overcook anything. Two: you will learn how your microwave works, how fast it cooks, how foods look and smell at the various stages of the cooking process. That knowledge will make you a more confident microwaver, and will persuade you – fingers crossed! – to put the machine to more and better use.

Microwave ovens differ in power output and in the size and shape of the oven's interior cavity. For this reason, timings are always approximate: there is no substitute for observation and experience with your particular oven.

vegetables

With vegetables, simplest is often best in the microwave. There are more elaborate dishes you can make, and they're good. But the prospect of fine fresh vegetables in a bowl with oil or butter, cooked for anything from two to ten minutes, is reason enough to buy one of the machines. I call the method micro-steaming.

basic methods

The basic micro-steaming method can be used with all of the following vegetables:

- Broccoli, in small florets and stalks peeled
- Butternut squash, halved or cut into small chunks
- Cabbage, finely shredded
- Carrots, sliced thick or thin
- Cauliflower, in small florets
- Celery, sliced thick or thin
- Courgettes, sliced thick or thin
- Fennel, thinly sliced
- Green beans, topped and tailed
- Mushrooms, whole, halved or in thick slices
- Okra, washed but untrimmed
- Peas, frozen or fresh
- Sweetcorn, fresh (in kernels) or frozen
- Tomatoes, whole

If you counter that you can steam the vegetables just as fast, I would reply that microwaving them:
- uses less water
- requires no preheating time for the water
- enables you to cook and serve in the same vessel, and
- is known to preserve more of the vitamin content than other cooking methods.

And, just to repeat what my wife points out: with the microwave, you don't need to worry about getting distracted and having the water boil away, thus potentially ruining your steamer.

Microwave cooking evaporates water at the cut surface of most vegetables, leading to dryness in the finished product. For this reason it's always good to coat the cut pieces with vegetable or extra virgin olive oil, or with butter, which will slow down evaporation. The vegetables can be served as soon as they're cooked, or left to be served at room temperature; they can also be reheated briefly if that suits your schedule.

The bowl has to be covered, needless to say. Barbara Kafka, author and doyenne of microwave cookery, uses clingfilm for this, and clingfilm works very well. Its disadvantage from a green point of view is that the clingfilm gets chucked away, and you can get through a lot of the stuff if you micro-steam frequently (as I do). It also has a practical disadvantage: if you stir the vegetables regularly, as I do, re-covering the bowl with the same sheet of clingfilm is difficult. If you use another sheet, you are adding more waste to landfill. My solution: a plate, with bottom facing downwards, placed on top of the bowl. It doesn't retain the steam quite as effectively as clingfilm, but it does well enough.

creamed courgettes

Cut 2 courgettes into thickish slices, around the thickness of the tip of your little finger. Put them in a bowl with 2 tablespoons single cream or extra virgin olive oil, or a generous knob of butter. Add a small splash (around 1 tablespoon) of water. Cook in 1-minute bursts for around 5 minutes, tossing after every minute. Season with salt and pepper, and you're done.

baked potatoes

You can't bake a potato properly in the microwave: the skin won't crisp up. What you can do, however, is use the magic box to cut the baking time by as much as 60 per cent. Just prick the potatoes in a few places with a fork, and microwave at full power, turning them over once. Cook until sizzling and too hot to handle without an oven glove, around 4–5 minutes per spud. Then pop them in the oven. They'll need around 30 minutes at 200°C/400°F/gas mark 6, as opposed to the normal 1 hour and 15 minutes.

sweetcorn from heaven

Really good, fresh ears of sweetcorn are an increasingly common sight in markets across the country. And cooking them in the microwave is easily the greenest option. It requires no water, does away with the lengthy time needed to bring the water to a boil, and doesn't leave you with a big pot to scrub clean. More important, it is by far the best way to cook sweetcorn. All the flavour and freshness is trapped inside the husks, because the ears are cooked without shucking. Sweetcorn cooked this way doesn't need butter. If it's good enough, it doesn't even need salt or pepper. The drawback: three ears is usually the most you can cook at a time. But the remainder can sit for a few minutes, or the sweetcorn can be served in instalments. Timings:

1 ear	around 3 minutes
2 ears	around 5–6 minutes
3 ears	around 9–12 minutes

grilled peppers in the microwave and a frying pan

If you are using the grill or the oven for something else, cook these peppers in the grill or oven as well. If not, try this method. The result isn't identical, but it's just as good, unless you need deep charring of the peppers.

Prick the peppers in a few places with a sharp knife and put them in any dish that will hold them comfortably. Cover it with a plate and cook at full power for around 4–5 minutes per pepper, checking regularly and turning once or twice. The peppers are done when they are soft.

The peppers can be eaten now, but they can also be used to make a low-energy version of grilled or roasted peppers. To finish cooking this way, put them in a frying pan lightly filmed with oil and cook, covered, over a medium-high heat until well blackened on the first side, around 2–3 minutes. Turn and cook the other side. They can now be peeled or just served as a rustic-type side dish.

garlic mushrooms

This is even better with wild mushrooms – here we've used shiitake and small St George's mushrooms.

Serves 4 as a side dish

- 350g small, pearly-white button mushrooms
- a good knob of unsalted butter
- 2 shallots or a small onion, finely chopped
- 2 medium garlic cloves, finely chopped
- a pinch of dried thyme
- 50ml dry white wine
- 100ml single cream
- a small handful of parsley or coriander leaves, finely chopped

Clean the mushrooms, trim off the stem-end but leave whole. Melt the butter in a glass bowl for around 30 seconds, then stir in the shallots or onion, garlic, thyme and wine. Cook at full power until the liquid has fully evaporated, around 1–2 minutes; stirring once is a good idea. Add the mushrooms, stir well, and cook in 1-minute bursts until just done, around 4–5 minutes. Stir in the cream, microwave again to heat through and serve immediately with the fresh herbs sprinkled on top.

peas with mint and lime

Serves 4 as a side dish

- 1 medium onion, finely chopped
- 2 tablespoons extra virgin olive oil
- 450g frozen peas
- 4–5 fresh mint leaves
- juice of 1 lime

Mix the onion with the oil in a large bowl and cook, uncovered, for 2 minutes (3 minutes if you want the onions to be meltingly soft). Mix in the peas, pour in a small splash of water, cover the bowl and cook for 5–8 minutes, stirring thoroughly every 2 minutes. To serve, tear the mint into tiny pieces and scatter on top. Squeeze the lime juice over and toss well.

my mother's sweet potatoes

If you are using the oven for something else, finishing the mashed sweet potatoes in a baking dish will give them a nice brown crust. NB: Ma Ehrlich got the recipe from a source she no longer remembers. If the author spots this unintentional pilfering, would he or she please contact me?

Serves 4 as a side dish

900g sweet potatoes
50–100ml maple syrup
   or clear honey
a very generous knob of butter
150ml milk
50g dried dates, stoned and
   coarsely chopped
juice of 1 lemon

Prick each potato a dozen times with a small, sharp knife. Place on a large plate and cook uncovered at full power for around 15 minutes, until perfectly soft when poked with that sharp knife. Leave to cool slightly, then peel and mash roughly in a large glass bowl; holding the potatoes in oven mitts will keep your hands from scorching.

Mix the potatoes with the remaining ingredients, adding enough maple syrup or honey to sweeten the mixture to your taste. Add more milk if the mixture seems dry – it should be the texture of mashed potatoes. Microwave at full power for 6–8 minutes, or until the potatoes are scaldingly hot. Note: this dish freezes very well. If you're going to freeze it, mix all the ingredients except the milk and cover tightly. When you're ready to serve, defrost thoroughly, add the milk and heat through.

broccoli with oyster sauce

Serves 4 as a side dish

1 large or 2 small heads
    of broccoli
1 tablespoon vegetable oil
2 tablespoons oyster sauce
1 large garlic clove,
    finely chopped
2 thick slices of peeled
    fresh ginger, finely chopped
2 tablespoons chicken
    stock or water
1 teaspoon sesame oil
toasted sesame seeds
    and spring onions (optional)

Cut the broccoli into florets and peel the stalks
if you want to use them. Cut thick stalks into quarters.

Toss in a large bowl with the oil and then the oyster
sauce, garlic, ginger and stock or water. Cover with a
plate and cook in 2-minute bursts, tossing well after each
burst. Total cooking time should be around 5–8 minutes,
depending on how soft you like your broccoli. When it's
done, toss with the sesame oil and serve immediately.

You could also sprinkle a teaspoon or so of lightly
toasted sesame seeds on top, and some finely chopped
spring onions.

Barbara Kafta's stewed okra

This is not just one of my favourite microwave dishes but one of my favourite
vegetable dishes made with any cooking method. The original recipe comes from
Barbara Kafka's *Microwave Gourmet*, but my version differs in several details.

Serves 4 as a side dish

1 large onion, thinly sliced
5 garlic cloves, coarsely
    chopped
1 small chilli, not too fiery
    (optional)
100ml extra virgin olive oil or
    vegetable oil
450g okra
400g tin chopped tomatoes
salt and freshly ground
    black pepper
lemon juice or red wine vinegar

Put the onion, garlic and chilli, if using, in a large bowl. Toss
well with the oil and cook until hot, 4–5 minutes. Toss once or
twice during cooking.

Now add the okra and toss well again. Cover with a plate
or some other lid (even clingfilm if you must) and cook until the
okra is starting to soften slightly, around 6 minutes. Toss every
couple of minutes. Add the tomatoes, toss again, and continue
cooking, tossing every couple of minutes, until the okra is
completely soft, around 10 minutes.

When the okra is done, season it with salt and pepper and a
generous squeeze of lemon juice or a shot of red wine vinegar.

tomatoes with balsamic vinaigrette and fresh herbs

This too has its distant origins in a Barbara Kafka recipe made with Chinese black beans and tamari (a type of soy sauce). I think this more conventional set of flavourings is more versatile, and it doesn't require access to exotic ingredients. The herbs are up to you. Basil, tarragon, mint and dill would all work well. Serve hot or at room temperature.

Serves 4 as a side dish

1–2 garlic cloves, finely chopped
2 tablespoons extra virgin olive oil
4 ripe tomatoes, cored and
    cut into 6 or 8 pieces
a very small handful of fresh
    herbs, leaves only, finely
    chopped ·
2 teaspoons balsamic vinegar
1 teaspoon lemon juice ·
salt and freshly ground
    black pepper

Put the garlic in a large bowl with 1 tablespoon of the olive oil. Microwave at full power for 30 seconds, then stir in the tomatoes and the herbs. Cover with a dinner plate and microwave at full power in 2-minute bursts, stirring well after each burst, until the tomatoes are very hot and soft but not collapsing, around 5–6 minutes.

In the meantime, whisk the remaining oil with the vinegar, lemon juice, and a good dose of salt and pepper. When the tomatoes are done, toss well with the vinaigrette and leave for a few minutes so the flavours have a chance to blend. And by the way: when you've finished with the tomatoes, save any leftover juice to use as the basis for another vinaigrette. As long as no one has licked the bowl, that is.

micro-braised chicory

1 head chicory per person,
    bases trimmed, and dry or
    blemished leaves removed
a small knob of butter per
    chicory head
100ml good chicken stock per
    chicory head
freshly ground black pepper

Lay the chicory flat in a deep dish and top each head with a knob of butter. Pour in the stock and grind on a little black pepper. (Cooked chicory is very pungent, so you should not need salt.) Microwave at full power for anything from 6–15 minutes, depending on the number of heads you are cooking. Two heads shouldn't need more than 7 minutes, 6–8 heads will need the full 15 minutes or perhaps a little more. Turning the heads in the middle of cooking is a good idea, but not strictly necessary.

summery aubergines

o called because they must be made with really red, ripe tomatoes if the
ish is to taste as it should. This recipe serves four as a side dish or two as
lunchtime main course, but to make it for more you need only multiply the
uantities and timing.

medium aubergine,
  around 375g
-5 slivers of garlic
tablespoons extra virgin olive oil
medium-sized tomato,
  ripe and sweet
alt and freshly ground
  black pepper
esh basil leaves, to serve

ave the aubergine whole, but make an
cision into its full length around 1–2cm
ep. Stick the garlic slivers into the
cision and put it in a bowl that will hold
easily. Drizzle around 1 teaspoon of
e oil along the length of the incision.

over with a plate and cook for 8–10
inutes, until the aubergine is steaming,
flated and soft. In the meantime,
seed the tomato and cut it into smallish
ce; you can peel it if you wish, but it
n't necessary.

hen the aubergine is done, cut along
e incision to open it out – don't cut it
ght through in half, just open it out like a
ook. Strew the tomato pieces inside and
ound the aubergine, pour in the rest of
e oil, and season it with salt and
pper. Cook for another 1–2 minutes,
til the tomato is hot but not mushy.
rinkle basil on top and around the
bergines for serving.

sauces

Sauces for pasta and other foods are a good way to start learning the resource-saving potential of the microwave. They almost always take less time to cook than they would in a pot or pan, and they allow you to cook the sauce in the bowl where the pasta will be served. That's one crusty pan you don't have to wash, which saves on water use, heating and washing-up liquid. Here are a few favourites of mine. If you learn the basic techniques, you will be able to adapt your favourite pasta sauces for the microwave.

Note: these quantities will sauce 500g of pasta, enough for 4 people.

sage and onion sauce

This is adapted from a recipe in Marcella Hazan's *Classic Italian Cookbook*. Hazan's recipe doesn't use sage, but that herb makes such a great partnership with onions that I think it's worth deviating from the great woman's advice.

around 50g butter
3–4 large onions, halved
　lengthwise and thinly sliced
salt and freshly ground
　black pepper
10–12 sage leaves, torn or cut
　in half
50ml dry white wine
extra virgin olive oil to taste

Put the butter in a large bowl and melt in the microwave for 30 seconds or so, then put in the onions, season with salt and pepper, and toss thoroughly. Cook at full power in 2-minute bursts, tossing well after each burst, until the onions are well softened and lightly coloured (around 10–12 minutes). When they seem to be about half-cooked, add the sage leaves and the wine, toss together and continue cooking.

When you toss with the pasta, add enough extra virgin olive oil to lubricate the dish well; this could be as little as 2 tablespoons or as much as 4, depending on how wet you like your pasta.

tomato sauce with pancetta

25g bacon or pancetta
tablespoon extra virgin olive oil
½ a dried red chilli, or ¼ teaspoon
  dried chilli flakes
2 small garlic cloves, finely chopped
stick of celery, finely chopped
small onion, finely chopped
teaspoon dried herbs – herbes de
  Provence, thyme or rosemary
2 x 400g tins good-quality
  plum tomatoes
teaspoon tomato purée
salt and freshly ground
  black pepper

Cut the bacon into thin shreds and put in a medium-sized glass bowl with the oil. Microwave at full power for 1 minute. Add the chilli, garlic, celery, onion and herbs. Microwave for 5–8 minutes, stirring every 2 minutes, until the vegetables are soft. (The one to test is the celery, which takes longer to sweat than the other ingredients.)

Now roughly chop the tomatoes (use scissors to snip them while still in the tin) and add them to the bowl with the tomato purée; season lightly with salt and pepper. Microwave for 8–10 minutes, stirring every 2 minutes, until the sauce is thick enough to suit your taste. It can now be kept for many hours. Just before the pasta is done, reheat the sauce for 1–2 minutes and mix with the pasta in the usual way.

Tip: For a meatless sauce, substitute an extra tablespoon of extra virgin olive oil for the bacon. This will be enough for 750g–1kg of dried pasta, so you should freeze what you don't use. It will be as good from the freezer as it is freshly made.

garlic and mushroom sauce

–4 plump garlic cloves, finely
  chopped or crushed
good knob of butter
large pinch of dried herbs –
  herbes de Provence, thyme or
  rosemary
00g button mushrooms,
  cleaned and sliced or (if very
  small) quartered
0ml dry white wine
alt and freshly ground black
  pepper
xtra virgin olive oil to taste
large handful of parsley, leaves
  only, finely chopped

Put the garlic, butter and dried herbs in a bowl and mash them up together with a fork. Microwave at full power for around 1 minute, just to get the garlic sizzling a little.

Put in the mushrooms and the wine and season with salt and pepper. Microwave in 1-minute bursts, tossing after each burst, until the mushrooms are hot and soft but still retaining a hint of al dente chewiness (around 4–5 minutes). When the pasta is cooked, toss with enough oil to lubricate it well and top with the parsley.

spaghetti all'aglio olio e peperoncini

In other words, with garlic, extra virgin olive oil and red chilli peppers. This is a quick sauce even in a frying pan, but in the microwave you eliminate the washing of that pan.

4 plump garlic cloves, thinly sliced
around 100ml extra virgin olive oil
1 teaspoon (or more if you like it
  spicy) dried chilli flakes
salt and freshly ground
  black pepper

Put the garlic and around 50ml of oil in a bowl with the chilli flakes and a little salt and pepper. Microwave at full power for 1 minute, just long enough to make the garlic smell really good

When the spaghetti is cooked, toss with the sauce and enough extra oil to lubricate it well. This sauce does not need grated Parmesan, though some people prefer it that way. Chopped parsley adds a little extra colour.

carbonara

This sauce cooks perfectly in the microwave. But success lies in using bacon or pancetta of the highest quality. Industrial bacon will not do.

4–5 thick slices of top-grade bacon
  or pancetta, rind removed
2 small or medium onions,
  sliced and cut into 5cm-long
  pieces
freshly ground black pepper
2 tablespoons dry white wine
3 large eggs
single or double cream to taste
a small handful of parsley,
  coarsely chopped
grated Parmesan

Snip the bacon or pancetta into thin shreds straight into a large bowl, using kitchen scissors. Cover it with a piece of paper or a dinner plate. Microwave at full power in 1-minute bursts, stirring each time to keep the bacon from sticking together, until it has started to render a lot of fat and is looking lightly browned, 3–4 minutes. Add the onions and plenty of black pepper (no salt), stir well, and cook again at full power in 1-minute bursts, stirring after each burst, until the onions are soft, around 5 minutes. Add the wine for the last minute or two of cooking.

Beat the eggs and add cream to taste. I think around 50ml is the perfect quantity, but you can use less or more for richer or lighter sauce. When the pasta is cooked, drain and add to the bowl with the onions. Stir well, then mix in the eggs and cream Top with the parsley and plenty of Parmesan.

fish

On the whole, as with vegetables, I don't think it's a good idea to try to get too complicated with microwaved fish. Some stew-type dishes can be made, and they are good, but the hassle of moving the pieces around just isn't worth it when conventional methods such as lidded frying (see page 32) work so well. Whole fish can also be cooked in the microwave, with careful preparation, but they too are done just as easily and almost as quickly in a pan. For me, microwaved fish is essentially steamed fish, with or without some extra flavourings. Here is the basic method I use most for microwaved fish.

simple salmon

Cut a thick salmon steak off the bone. Put in a flat-bottomed dish, seasoning as you like, and cover with a plate. Microwave at full power for 1 minute. Check its progress, then cook for another 30–90 seconds. Serve with lidded beans (page 48) and a lemon wedge.

You can cook as many steaks as your microwave oven will hold, as long as they're in a single layer. Four steaks is probably the practical maximum, however. Just remember that you will need an extra 2–3 minutes for every extra steak.

ariations for steamed fish

1 Cut thin slices of unwaxed lemon and put one underneath each steak. Put another one on top.

2 Put a splash of dry white wine in the dish with the fish. When the fish is cooked, remove to serving plates and whisk in a bit of double cream or crème fraîche and finely chopped fresh herbs to make a little sauce.

3 Cook the fish with butter smeared lightly on both sides, to add richness to the juices.

more complicated fish

If you're cooking more complicated fishy dishes in the microwave, which will require stirring, you're well advised to use very firm-fleshed fish or shellfish. Chunks of anything soft will tend to break up on stirring.

quick fish curry

Even though I generally like fish simply cooked in the microwave, certain stewy preparations are also very well suited to the magic box. Every bit of cooking can be done in a glass bowl, so there's only one dish to wash up. And the whole thing takes just minutes from beginning to end. Use any sustainable but firm-fleshe white fish, such as pollock, gurnard or huss. These quantities will serve four with a side dish of plain boiled rice. And note: if you have a favourite fish curry recipe, you can adapt it for the microwave using this basic method.

Serves 4–6

1 medium onion, coarsely chopped
2–3 garlic cloves, finely chopped
a small knob of fresh ginger,
   peeled and finely chopped
2 tablespoons vegetable oil
1 cardamom pod
1–2 tablespoons curry powder,
   homemade or commercial
around 1.2kg fish, cut into chunks
   or strips around 2.5cm thick
around 200ml Greek or Bio yogurt
a small handful of fresh coriander
   leaves, chopped

Put the onion, garlic, ginger and oil in a large bowl and stir well to mix. Microwave at full power in 1-minute bursts until the mixture is lightly coloured and extremely fragrant, around 2 minutes. Now add the cardamom pod and curry powder, and microwave again for another minute. Add the fish, with 100ml water, and stir well to coat every piece with the onion-spice mixture.

Microwave for 6–7 minutes more, stirring thoroughly every minute or two, until the fish is just cooked. Mix in enough yogurt to make the dish wet but not too watery, and cook again on a low to medium power just to heat it through thoroughly. Add the coriander and serve immediately.

gambas al ajillo

Small to medium-sized prawns cook well in the microwave as long as you stir them regularly – especially if you're cooking more than a couple of hundred grams' worth. This is the microwave adaptation of one of the classic dishes of Spain. If the prawns have their heads on, use the larger weight.

Serves 2

300–450g small or medium
　prawns, shell on
2 small garlic cloves, finely chopped
a pinch to ½ teaspoon of
　dried chilli flakes
a large pinch of Spanish
　sweet paprika
2 tablespoons extra virgin olive oil
2 teaspoons dry white wine

Make sure the prawns are completely defrosted if they have been frozen. Put the garlic, chilli flakes, paprika, oil and wine in a glass bowl large enough to hold the prawns comfortably. Microwave at full power for around 30 seconds, just long enough to make the garlic smell fragrant, then put in the prawns and toss thoroughly to coat them with oil. Microwave at full power in 1-minute bursts, tossing well after every burst. Check each time you toss to locate any prawns that are less cooked than the rest (they retain more of their grey colour, unlike the pink of the cooked ones), and move them to the edge of the prawn-mass in the bowl.

Total cooking time should be around 4–5 minutes, with 1 minute of resting when they're done. Serve with rice or good bread.

squid and celery 'stir-fry'

If you have some leftover rice that has been kept in the fridge for no more than a couple of days, you can add a maximum of around 250g when you put in the celery.

Serves 2

2–3 slices of peeled fresh ginger, shredded
1 garlic clove, shredded
1 dried red chilli, crumbled
2–3 spring onions, halved lengthwise and cut into 5cm pieces
1 teaspoon peanut oil
350g cleaned squid tubes (uncleaned weight 500g), cut into bite-sized pieces
4–5 sticks of celery, thinly sliced at an angle
2 tablespoons soy sauce
2 tablespoons red wine vinegar
1 teaspoon sesame oil

Mix the ginger, garlic, chilli, one of the spring onions and the peanut oil in a bowl large enough to accommodate the squid and celery. Toss well and cook at full power for 1 minute, just to get the garlic smelling fragrant, then add the squid and cook in 1-minute bursts, stirring after each burst, until the squid seems to be half-cooked, 2–3 minutes. Add the celery, and rice, if using.

Toss well and cook in 1-minute bursts, stirring after each burst, until the celery is very hot but still quite crunchy, around 2–3 minutes. Toss with the soy sauce, vinegar and sesame oil and top with the remaining spring onions. Serve immediately, with boiled rice if you haven't used leftover rice in the squid.

gurnard in tomato sauce

Pollack or whiting can be substituted here, or any other sustainable white fish.

Serves 4

4 gurnard fillets (from a whole
  fish if big, from 2 if smaller)
1 plump garlic clove, finely chopped
1 tablespoon extra virgin olive oil
a small handful of coriander leaves,
  coarsely chopped
300ml homemade tomato sauce
  (see page 168)

Ask your fishmonger to bone out the fish through the belly, so that the 2 fillets are attached at the back. Scrape the blood from the cavity and snip off the fins.

Mix the garlic with the oil in a bowl large enough to hold the fish. Cook for 1 minute and leave to cool for a minute or so, then mix in the coriander. Spread this mixture inside the fish and roll up the flaps; secure with toothpicks and pour in the tomato sauce.

Cook the fish at full power for 7–8 minutes and leave to rest for at least 5 minutes to complete the cooking. Serve with rice or potatoes, and be sure to spoon out all the sauce.

poultry

The microwave's advantages with poultry are limited if you want the bird to brown. Microwave ovens can brown food under certain circumstances, but it's easier in a lidded pan (see page 32) than in the microwave. The recipes here produce an effect that's more akin to steaming or braising than to sautéing or stir-frying. They can be made with the skin on or off, but remember that the skin is sort of useless if it doesn't get brown and crisp.

If you find yourself in need of a quick dinner but the only edibles are frozen chicken pieces, fear not. They can be defrosted and part-cooked in the microwave, then finished in a lidded pan. But the serious health-warning: make sure that the pieces are well cooked when they come out of the pan. Salmonella and other dangers may lurk in under-cooked chicken. Just make sure the chicken pieces are sizzling-hot when you take them out of the microwave.

chicken curry for one

This is a really nice little dish, requiring minimal work, and it is both fast and easy enough to keep solitary eaters from eating a boiled egg or a ready-meal for dinner. To make it for two, just double the ingredients and the cooking time. If you don't want to go to the trouble of adding spices individually, use best-quality curry powder. It will still be better than a ready-meal.

1 thick slice of onion, coarsely chopped
2 tablespoons vegetable oil
1 garlic clove, finely chopped
2 thin slices of peeled fresh ginger, finely chopped
a small pinch each of ground cumin, ground coriander, black mustard seeds and fenugreek
chilli powder or dried chilli flakes to taste
1 teaspoon cornflour
1 tablespoon Greek or Bio yogurt, plus extra, to serve
250g skinless, boneless chicken, in chunks or strips
sprig of fresh coriander, to serve

Put the onion in a deep bowl with the vegetable oil and toss them together. Microwave at full power for 1 minute, then add the garlic and ginger and microwave again for 1 minute. Stir in the spices and cook for another 30 seconds.

Mix the cornflour into the spice mixture, then the yogurt, then the chicken. Microwave at full power for 4–5 minutes, stirring after every minute. Serve with extra yogurt and coriander. If you can't be bothered to cook rice just for yourself, a piece of bread will do for mopping up the spicy gravy.

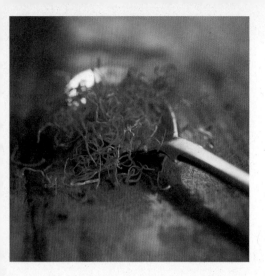

chicken in a pot
with saffron cream

This is an indulgent but simple one-pot dinner. The ideal herb is tarragon, but parsley will do just fine. Serve with a plainly cooked vegetable such as green beans or broccoli.

Serves 4

100ml double cream
a large pinch of saffron
1 large garlic clove, crushed or finely chopped
500g maincrop potatoes, peeled
   and cut into chunks
150ml chicken stock, or a 50-50
   mix of stock and dry white wine
salt and freshly ground black pepper
4–8 chicken thighs (depending on
   their size), skinned if you wish
1 large onion, cut into chunks
6–8 sprigs of tarragon or a
   small handful of parsley leaves,
   coarsely chopped

Put the cream, saffron and garlic in a small jug and heat at full power in 1-minute bursts until the cream is hot. Take care not to let it boil, or it will froth over the sides of the jug. Leave to infuse while you do the rest of the cooking.

Put the potatoes and liquid in a large bowl and toss well with salt and pepper. Cover the bowl and cook at full power for around 4 minutes, just until the liquid is starting to show signs of boiling. Now add the chicken and onion, toss well, and continue cooking for another 10–12 minutes, until the chicken is barely cooked and the potatoes are fully softened. Add the infused cream and cook for another 1–2 minutes, until the liquid is bubbling lightly. Stir in the herbs, check the seasoning and serve.

defrosting tips

Defrosting isn't cooking, but it is still something with which the microwave can help out in very useful ways. Here are a few tips.

• Use power settings lower than full power: they do the job more efficiently. Try starting at medium power and then switching to low for a couple of minutes. Your oven may have symbols for 'automatic' defrosting levels, and you may find these useful, but don't follow them slavishly.

• Defrost using 1- to 2-minute bursts, checking after each burst and using a lower power once the food has started to soften.

• Don't let the food get hot or it will start to cook on the outside before the inside is defrosted. If it gets hot, stop immediately. Food you're heating in its freezer wrapper can be cooled under cold water from the tap.

• If you're defrosting meat, turn it regularly.

• Try to plan in advance: start the defrosting at least an hour or so before you need to cook, if possible, so defrosting can finish at room temperature.

meat

With meat, as with poultry, the difficulty of obtaining browning reactions in meat limits what you can do with it in the microwave. But that shouldn't eliminate it from consideration. The microwave is an excellent way to precook small joints for finishing in a frying pan, giving you something that's akin to a roast dinner in a matter of minutes. You can also speed up the cooking of larger joints destined for the oven, which yields tremendous savings in energy. And on its own, it can cook certain meats very successfully. Here are examples of all three methods.

small joints

If you're cooking just for two or three people, conventional roasting is an energy-intensive proposition. It means turning on the oven to cook a pound or so of meat.

There is an alternative, ideally suited to smaller joints. Namely: cook your joint in the microwave, then brown it quickly for colour. A smallish joint is best because microwave energy penetrates food only to a depth of around 2.5cm, so heat is concentrated near the surface. With a small joint, heat spreads to the centre while the meat is resting and the pan is preheating.

The best cuts are all from pork or lamb.
• For pork: rolled loin or shoulder (rind removed, as it will not turn to crackling).
• For lamb: rump, rolled loin, hunk of shoulder, thin end of the leg. It shouldn't be more than around 10cm thick at its thickest point.

It's important to have the meat at true room temperature so the microwave doesn't have to take the chill out of a fridge-cold centre. And please remember that your timings may differ slightly from mine, as no two microwave ovens are exactly alike. The timings here are a guideline only. Use an instant-read probe thermometer to gauge doneness. Lamb should be around 63°C/145°F, pork around 66°C/150°F.

With those caveats in mind, here's the procedure.

Put the meat in a suitable bowl and microwave at around three-quarter power for around 8–10 minutes, turning once. When done, drain well (reserving the juices) and heat some vegetable oil in a heavy pan. Brown the meat well all over, around 5 minutes. While it's resting before its date with the carving knife, deglaze the pan with the reserved microwaved juices to make gravy.

arge joints

Larger pieces of meat can also be cooked in this two-step method, but the aims and procedure are different. You will never get microwave energy to penetrate deep into the centre of a 15cm-thick leg of lamb or rolled rib of beef, but you can cut the cooking time in the oven by starting the joint in the microwave.
• While the oven is preheating, microwave at full power. If your oven is operating efficiently, the preheating should take around 10 minutes, and that's the right amount of time to cook the meat in the microwave.
• Transfer to a roasting tin as soon as you take the meat out of the microwave, season and roast.

There's no hard-and-fast rule for timing the joint in the oven, but you can figure on cutting at least 30 minutes off the normal roasting time.

sliced beef casserole

This is another recipe from Barbara Kafka, who based her dish on a recipe from Elizabeth David. I have hardly changed a thing in it, because it is already so good. Chuck is the cut that Kafka calls for. If your butcher can't help you with that, use another cut from the shoulder. Since this is a party dish, I have given it (as Kafka does) in quantities that will serve 6–8.

1 medium onion, cut into
    small chunks
3 big carrots, cut into 1cm dice
2 large strips of orange zest
6 garlic cloves, roughly chopped
a good knob of butter
1 bay leaf
½ teaspoon dried thyme
1.5kg braising beef, sliced around
    1.5cm thick
3 rashers of bacon
150ml chicken or beef stock
225ml red wine
75ml brandy (optional but
    very good)

Mix the onion, carrots, orange zest and garlic in a flat-bottomed dish large enough to hold the beef comfortably; a large soufflé dish is perfect. Add a splash of water and cook briefly, just to heat everything a little, then stir in the butter and continue cooking until very hot, around 3 minutes. Stir in the bay leaf and thyme.

Layer half of the beef slices in the bottom of the dish, overlapping them like the tiles on a roof.

Lay the bacon on top, then layer in the remaining beef. Pour on the stock, wine and brandy, if using, and cover with a plate or a sheet of clingfilm; clingfilm works well in this because of the efficiency with which it traps steam. Cook for 10 minutes at full power, then uncover and give a gentle stir, trying not to disturb the neat slices more than necessary. Re-cover and cook again at full power for another 3–4 minutes, until the dish is bubbling enthusiastically.

This dish, like nearly all meat casseroles, greatly benefits from being cooked in advance, left to cool, and then reheated just before serving.

spicy meat loaf
with thai flavours

This is an unusual meat loaf, and deeply delicious if I say so myself.
Needless to say, you can omit the exotica and make something that's
more conventionally seasoned. Get the butcher to mince both meats
through the medium plate.

Serves 4–6

small onions (around 350g),
  coarsely chopped
large garlic cloves, finely chopped
large piece of peeled fresh ginger,
  finely chopped
lemongrass stalk, finely chopped
0 kaffir lime leaves, finely shredded
small red chilli, deseeded
  and finely chopped
tablespoons vegetable oil
00g cubed beef, pork or dark-meat
  chicken, minced (see above)
00g streaky bacon
5g fresh breadcrumbs
eggs
tablespoon soy sauce
tablespoon Thai fish sauce,
  or nam pla
tablespoon red wine vinegar
eshly ground black pepper

Put the onions, garlic, ginger, lemongrass, lime leaves and
chilli in a bowl with the oil and microwave gently on a
low-moderate setting until soft, 3–4 minutes, then leave to
cool. Meanwhile, put the remaining ingredients in
a large mixing bowl.

When the onions are cool, blend everything thoroughly
with your (clean) hands. Season with plenty of black
pepper but just a little salt, since the bacon, soy sauce
and fish sauce are already salty. Microwave a spoonful to
test for seasoning; you may feel that extra salt is called for.
If the loaf is to be served cold, remember that seasonings
lose some of their pungency when they cool off.

Pack the mixture into a ring mould (ideal) or a squarish,
non-metallic loaf tin, taking special care to push it into the
corners, if using a square tin, and tapping firmly several
times to settle it. Cook uncovered, at full power, for
around 10–15 minutes, until the centre of the loaf feels
firm to the touch and a meat thermometer gives a reading
of 63°C/145°F. Leave for 15 minutes before serving. If
serving cold, leave for 30 minutes before pouring off the
liquid (which should be saved for soup or gravy), then
cover loosely and leave until quite cool before covering
tightly and refrigerating until needed (24 hours maximum).

little incidentals

One of the best uses for the microwave is making quick accompaniments for a meal being cooked elsewhere in the kitchen. Too substantial to be called garnishes, too small to be called side dishes, they are Little Incidentals in my book. I make them with whatever happens to be lying around, and they can serve as a miniature side dish, or as a nibble to eat while the meal is cooking.

cherry tomatoes

Put the tomatoes in a shallow dish that holds them in a single layer. Coat with extra virgin olive oil and a little vinegar. Add a bit of chopped garlic or onion or spring onion. Microwave at full power for 1–3 minutes, stirring once or twice; the exact timing will depend on the number of tomatoes, but the aim is to heat and soften rather than cook to a full-blown saucy mush. Serve on little squares of toast.

pure mushrooms

I love mushrooms, and enjoy eating them in this completely unadorned form: heated through just to the point of al dente softness, with no seasoning. To do it: wipe them clean and put in a bowl just large enough to hold them. Microwave at full power for 1 minute at a time, stirring well after each minute, until they are hot and soft. This shouldn't take more than 2 minutes for a small number of mushrooms, 4 minutes for larger quantities. The juice they express is pure mushroom essence; don't throw it away. If you want, season them with coarse salt. I don't bother.

instant chorizo

Slice the chorizo thinly and put in a single layer on a microwave-safe plate with a paper towel to cover. Cook at full power for 1 minute at a time, until sizzling hot. Mop up any excess fat with the paper towel, then tip into a small serving bowl.

salmon, lemon, dill

Cut the thin trimmings from salmon steaks or fillets into little chunks. Slice a lemon very thinly and cut off the skin and pith, then cut the slices into small pieces – you need one piece for every chunk of salmon. Put a small sprig of dill on each chunk of salmon, season with black pepper, then attach a piece of lemon to each salmon piece with a toothpick. Put them on a microwave-safe serving plate in a single layer and microwave at full power until the salmon is warm but not fully cooked, 1–3 minutes depending on how many pieces there are.

4. pressure cookers

Please don't skip this chapter! I'm serious. I love pressure cookers, and consider them to be an essential part of any Green Kitchen. *Times* reader Avril Allan, whose words are quoted opposite, has just the right idea. Many of your favourite oven- and saucepan-cooked dishes can be produced beautifully in the pressure cooker, with just a little adaptation needed.

Pressure cookers have been around for decades, and maybe that's part of their image problem: they seem to many home cooks like an old-fashioned piece of equipment, something that your mother or grandmother used. Even if that's true, you shouldn't let image get in the way of your embracing these truly remarkable pots. They speed up cooking by a factor of two, three or even four. And you don't have to compromise at all in quality.

Pressure cookers cook faster than normal pans because water boils at a higher temperature when it's under pressure. The pressure cooker has a tight seal around its rim which doesn't allow steam to escape, and as the steam builds up inside – typically to a pressure of 15psi (pounds per square inch) – it raises the temperature in the pot to around 125°C (250°F). Steam forces its way into the food, cooking it much faster than boiling water.

'I just adapt the recipe and bung everything in at once with some water – yum yum.'

AVRIL ALLAN

don't they explode?

With all that pressure building up inside, the pot would bulge and eventually explode without a safety valve to vent the steam once full pressure is reached. In early pressure cookers, the valve was fairly primitive and susceptible to blockages by food particles.

Modern versions have valves that are safer and easier to operate, and they also have multiple safety mechanisms to prevent excessive build-up of steam. They still need occasional attention to make sure the valve isn't blocked – check the manufacturer's instructions – but on safety grounds there is nothing to fear from them.

feeding the pot

Whenever you use a pressure cooker, you have to ensure that it isn't filled either too little or too much. Check the instructions that come with your cooker and follow them. This is especially important when it comes to liquid minimums, which are needed to avoid evaporation of the water and the catching of food on the bottom of the pot. It's also important to avoid overfilling with foods that expand during cooking, such as rice and pulses. As a general rule, you will need at least 250ml of liquid. And you shouldn't fill the pot more than halfway with foods that expand greatly. But again: check the manufacturer's instructions.

what can you cook in a pressure cooker?

I am still trying to figure out the answer to that question, but at the moment the more pertinent question seems to be: what can't you cook? The more I use my pressure cooker, the more I discover its possibilities. Of course, there is one thing the pressure cooker won't do – keep a crisp, browned crust on a piece of meat. But that's the case in any predominantly moist cooking environment.

Excluding that limitation, the list of candidates for pressure is almost endless. Meats that you would ordinarily braise; pulses and selected grains; most types of vegetable; complicated dishes and ultra simple ones – all of these are suitable. The tips and recipes here are just a selection of the possibilities that I have found most fruitful. When you buy your own pressure cooker and really start working with it, you will find your own.

question of release

On most modern pressure cookers, the controls make it impossible to open the pan once full pressure has been reached. There's a good reason for this: if you took the top off when the built-up steam was still trapped inside, you'd burn your hands and forearms. Only when the pressure has dropped to a safe level can the lid be released. There are two ways to vent the steam:

• Let it vent slowly on its own, which takes around 10 minutes.
• Open the vent for faster release, producing an amazing whoosh of billowing steam. If you aim this at the splashback on your hob, you can use it to clean off the surface.

If you go for the slow option, the food will continue cooking the whole while. This is a form of residual heat, one of the Green Kitchen's greatest tools for energy-saving. That pressurised steam is a very powerful form of cooking. But slow release isn't suitable for all dishes. If you cook green vegetables, even a minute of active cooking will turn them soft with slow release. For al dente vegetables, fast release is essential. In all the recipes here I specify which method to use.

note on timing and liquid

Pressure cookers don't like it when you put too little liquid in them. This makes them build up insufficient steam and thus cook the food more slowly than you expect. If in doubt, or while you're in the learning phase, you shouldn't be afraid to vent the steam immediately and check on doneness. If the food needs more cooking time, just clamp the lid back on and bring it up to full pressure again.

This doesn't take long, so you're not wasting much energy. After a while, your estimates as to timing will become more accurate. And a cardinal rule: if in doubt, use more liquid. The more you use, the more steam pressure there will be and the faster the food will cook. Excess liquid will be full of flavour; what you don't use immediately will form the basis of another good dish.

soup

Soup is a natural for the pressure cooker. Whatever you cook to al dente firmness in the pressure cooker can also be cooked to soothing, melting softness. It takes nothing more than a little extra time, which in turn means less worry about getting the timings exactly right. And you can combine slower-cooking vegetables with longer-cooking vegetables because they'll both end up being soft.

Some pressure cooker soup recipes call for cooking the ingredients in the liquid, but that's not always the best way forward. Steaming is often a better option, for the simple reason that it gives so much more flexibility. If you want to add just a little liquid to make the soup, you can. If you want more liquid, you can do that too. You can make it with all stock, all milk, or a combination. If you want to pull out some of the vegetables for another use, or for keeping whole if you're puréeing the rest, it's easier with the steamer insert.

What follows is a series of soups, all made using exactly the same method. I describe the method opposite, with the recipes containing just a list of ingredients. Add salt and pepper at the end as you see fit. Where there's a difference in method between the master recipe and another one, it is described where appropriate.

Finally: please treat these recipes as a beginning for your own experiments. If you have a favourite soup, you can adapt it to the pressure cooker using my suggestions as a model.

simple steamed soups

he soupy template

Cut up all the vegetables into pieces 1–1.5cm thick; this is the ideal size for cooking speedily, and is also good whether you are going to purée them or leave them whole. Put everything in the steamer basket of the pressure cooker with at least 750ml of water in the bottom of the pot. (But follow the manufacturer's instructions if in doubt.) Bring up to full pressure and cook for 10 minutes, then turn off the heat and vent the steam gradually.

When the vegetables are cooked, you can leave them whole or purée them. If you're leaving them whole, simply lift out the steamer basket and plonk the vegetables back into the pressure cooker. Add liquid, reheat quickly, and you're ready to eat.

The greenest way to purée the vegetables is in a mechanical device – such as a mouli-légumes – rather than an electric blender. Treat yourself to the electricity use: it's just so much easier.

eek and potato soup

Serves 2

-4 medium-sized leeks,
  white parts only
large baking potato

This needs around 450ml of liquid, chicken stock by preference but water if that's all you have. Milk will also do just fine. Chopped chives are the perfect garnish (à la vichyssoise), and you can expand on that theme by putting a little cream in each serving bowl.

leek and cauliflower soup

Serves 4

250g leeks
100g potatoes
1 medium cauliflower,
    around 600g trimmed weight

This needs around 1 litre of liquid. Water and milk are probably the ideal combination. This is a mild-flavoured soup, so will need ample seasoning with salt and pepper. White pepper looks nicer than black.

cabbage soup with bacon

A hearty winter soup if ever there was one: perfect for a cold-weather lunch.

Serves 4–6

a good-sized hunk of bacon
    or pancetta, around 150–250g,
    or the equivalent amount in
    bacon rashers
1 large head of white or
    Savoy cabbage
2 large carrots
4 garlic cloves

This needs around 1 litre of chicken or vegetable stock. It shouldn't be puréed.

courgette soup with lemongrass

serves 4

450g courgettes
250g onions
250g potatoes
1 lemongrass stalk, outer layers
    removed and the remainder
    very finely chopped

This needs around 450ml of liquid, chicken stock by preference but water if that's all you have. Milk will also do just fine. Chopped chives are the perfect garnish (à la vichyssoise), and you can expand on that theme by putting a little cream in each serving bowl.

a few more complicated soups

hearty vegetable soup

Double-cooking in the pressure cooker is perfectly suited for this dish. Indeed, I can't think of a better use for it, as the principle is so wonderfully flexible. You cook some meaty bones with aromatic ingredients until the meat is just soft enough to cut off the bones, then re-cook it with fresh aromatics and vegetables. The result is a deeply flavoured soup in which everything is cooked perfectly. A combination of different meats can be used if this suits you.

Serves 4

First cooking
500–900g bones with some meat on them, e.g. pig's trotters, beef ribs, pork ribs, neck of lamb, chicken backs, wings or carcasses
3–4 garlic cloves, unpeeled
2 sticks of celery, cut into large chunks
2 carrots, cut into large chunks
1 medium onion, cut into large chunks
4–5 new potatoes
dried herbs of your choice, such as herbes de Provence
salt and freshly ground black pepper

Final cooking
2 sticks of celery, cut into chunks
2 carrots, cut into chunks
1 medium onion, cut into chunks
chopped fresh parsley, coriander or dill, to finish

Put the bones in the pressure cooker with the garlic, celery, carrots, onion and potatoes. Add your chosen herbs, a little salt and lots of pepper. Put in enough liquid – water is fine, some dry white wine would make a great addition – just to cover the bones. Clamp the lid on and bring up to full pressure, then turn the heat down and cook for 20 minutes. Turn the heat off and leave until you can take the lid off.

Remove everything except the potatoes, using a slotted spoon. Compost the vegetable matter, if possible. Cut each potato in half. Pull the meat off the bones, trimming away visible fat, and return the meat to the pot. Leaving it in fairly large chunks or shreds is ideal, but don't worry if there are scrappy bits in there.

Add the second batch of celery, carrots and onion to the pot. Top up with liquid to cover everything, if you need to. Clamp the lid back on and bring to full pressure, then cook for another 5 minutes. Turn off the heat and leave until you can take the lid off. The vegetables should be very soft and all the flavours well blended. Season to taste, top with the chopped herbs and serve.

potato and rocket soup

After eating this rustic soup at an heroically overpriced restaurant in London,
I found a recipe for it in Marcella Hazan's *Second Classic Italian Cookbook*.
Her version is just as good as the restaurant's, and mine adapts it in several
ways. Most important: Hazan cooks the rocket for 15 or so minutes, but I prefer
to keep more of its flavour so I treat it more gently. You can use watercress if
there's no rocket around, though you should make sure to use the leaves only.

Serves 4

4 big potatoes, peeled and cut
　　into 1cm dice
water or stock (cube is fine) to taste
salt and freshly ground black pepper
100g rocket or watercress,
　　coarsely chopped
a thick slice of good bread
　　per person (stale is fine)
good extra virgin olive oil, to serve

Add water to the pressure cooker according to the
manufacturer's instructions. Put the potatoes in the steamer
insert, bring up to full pressure, and steam for 5 minutes.
Turn off the heat and cool until the lid can be removed.

While the pot is still hot, turn the heat back on to low and
gradually put in enough liquid to reach the consistency you
like. This quantity of potato could take a litre of water or even
more, if you want a thin soup. Season generously with salt
pepper. Stir in the green stuff, put the bread slices in the po
turn the heat off, and leave, covered, for 10 minutes.

When the bread is thoroughly soaked but not falling to bits,
serve the soup with a good shot of oil – the best you've
got – squirted into each bowl.

butternut and carrot soup

Serves 4

½ butternut squash
4 small carrots, chopped
2 small onions, chopped
1 small potato, peeled and chopped
2 thin slices of peeled, fresh ginger
2 garlic cloves, peeled and chopped
800ml stock (a cube will do fine)
salt and freshly ground black pepper

Precook the squash in the pressure cooker, giving it 5 minute
from the time full pressure is reached, or in the microwave fo
6–8 minutes. When it's cool enough to handle, scoop the fle
out of the skin, using a large spoon.

Put everything in the pressure cooker with a good dose of sa
and pepper. Clamp the lid on, bring to full pressure and coo
for 10 minutes. Use gradual release. When the lid can be ta
off and the soup has cooled a bit, purée with a hand blende
This can be refrigerated for a couple of days.

chicken, barley
and bacon soup

his is almost a meal in itself – certainly a heartily satisfying Saturday lunch after
 morning of gardening or walking on a chilly day. Start putting the soup
)gether at least 1½ hours before serving time, so the barley can soak and the
ressure can release gradually. Suggestion: cook it in the morning and reheat
ıst before lunch. Another suggestion: using frozen chicken pieces is ideal, so
ey'll be fully cooked but not totally mushy. Suggestion number three: if you
ave some scraps of leftover ham, use them instead of the bacon.

erves 4

50g pot barley, soaked in a few
 changes of cold water for a total
 of 20 minutes
)0g frozen chicken wings, thighs
 or drumsticks
-6 slices of streaky bacon,
 smoked if possible
 sticks of celery, cut into chunks
-3 carrots, cut into chunks
 bay leaf
teaspoon fennel seeds
teaspoon herbes de Provence
 or dried thyme
ılt and freshly ground black pepper

Drain the barley and give it a final rinse. Plonk into the pressure
cooker with the remaining ingredients plus a very little salt and
quite a lot of pepper. Fill with water just to cover by 2–3cm,
clamp on the lid, bring to full pressure and cook for 20
minutes. Turn the heat off and use gradual pressure release.

Chicken being rather fatty nowadays, this soup will benefit from
degreasing. When that's done, heat it up gently and test the
seasoning. You may want to dilute the broth with water if it
needs to feed more people or if it's so flavourful it can simply
take the dilution.

chicken soup
with new season's garlic

This is based on a soup recipe in Fergus Henderson's *Nose to Tail Cooking*, one of the best cookbooks of recent years. Henderson tells us to purée or sieve the garlic into the soup after cooking; I like this more rustic approach, though your guests will have to be true garlic-lovers to appreciate it. The dish couldn't be simpler, but it does require (a) top-notch homemade chicken stock and (b) the mild, sweet garlic of spring.

Serves 4–6

4–6 whole heads of new season's
   garlic, unpeeled but with the
   papery outer layers of husk
   removed
1 litre best chicken stock
salt and freshly ground black pepper
a large handful of parsley,
   finely chopped
good bread for serving, toasted

Put the garlic and stock in the pressure cooker with salt and pepper to taste. Clamp on the lid and bring to full pressure, then cook for 5 minutes. Turn off the heat and let the steam vent gradually.

To serve, divide the garlicky stock between heated serving bowls and sprinkle on some parsley. Put a whole head of garlic on each side plate, each of which should have a freshly toasted slice of bread. Your guests pick cloves of garlic off the head, slip them onto the toast (or into their mouths), and chew with a spoonful of stock in each mouthful.

vegetables

I used to use a steamer for cooking vegetables; now I use the pressure cooker. Pressure cookers do the job faster, and while you have to watch the timing much more carefully if you don't want them to overcook, that extra effort is worth it for the enormous gain in speed. And the pressure cooker can accommodate a larger quantity than all but the most capacious steamers, so it's ideal when you're cooking for a crowd.

The first approach to vegetables is the basic one: cooking them in a way that achieves the same effect as boiling or steaming. To do it, you will need a pressure cooker with a steamer insert. As far as I can tell, most new pressure cookers have such an insert so you're all set. If yours does not, you can improvise with the steamer insert from another pot, upended if necessary, or with a free-standing insert such as the type that folds out like an iris.

Every pressure cooker comes with instructions on use, which include a specified minimum of water to use when you're steaming. The reason: you don't want the water to cook down too far, damaging the pot or causing a serious loss of pressure. From my own experience, the minimum errs on the side of caution: there's water aplenty left in the pot after a few minutes of steaming. But stick by the rules. It just isn't worth taking a chance.

cooking times

Here are the cooking times that I've established for my own pressure cooker, all for vegetables cut into normal-sized serving pieces. Yours may differ slightly, and you will have to figure it out through trial and error – though your pressure cooker is likely to include some recipes which will guide you. In all cases, the timings are for al dente veg.

A final note: the water used for steaming is useful stuff. It will have a pronounced taste of whatever you cooked over it, and can be added to soup, sauces and stews.

Vegetable	Cooking time	Release
Cabbage	2 minutes	Immediate
Sprouts	2 minutes	Immediate
Carrots	3 minutes	Immediate
Celery	2 minutes	Immediate
Fennel	2 minutes	Immediate
Green beans	2 minutes	Immediate
Leeks	2 minutes	Immediate
Parsnips	5 minutes	Immediate
Broccoli	1 minute	Immediate
Peas	1 minute	Immediate

potatoes under pressure

The pressure cooker performs several small miracles
with the humble potato.

small new potatoes

Wash thoroughly but leave whole and unpeeled. Add water to the pressure
cooker according to the manufacturer's instructions. Put the potatoes in the steamer
insert. Bring up to full pressure and cook for 5 minutes. Turn off the heat and cool
until the lid can be removed.

larger potatoes, e.g. cyprus

Wash thoroughly but leave whole and unpeeled. Add water to the pressure
cooker according to the manufacturer's instructions. Put the potatoes in the steamer
insert. Bring up to full pressure and cook for 20 minutes. Turn off the heat and
cool until the lid can be removed.

mash

Add water to the pressure cooker according to the manufacturer's instructions. Peel
the potatoes, cut into chunks around 2.5cm thick and put them in the steamer
insert. Bring up to full pressure and cook for 5 minutes. Turn off the heat and cool
until the lid can be removed.

other vegetable dishes

teamed spring greens

sometimes boring vegetable made exciting. Instead of turning the greens
ut into a serving bowl, you can invert the steamer insert on a plate and
rve them in an elegant-looking mound.

rves 4–6 as a side dish

3 heads of spring greens
(around 1kg in total), trimmed,
:ored and sliced as thickly
is you like
easpoon each of whole cumin
seeds, coriander seeds and
enugreek
jarlic cloves, finely chopped
t and freshly ground black pepper
jood knob of butter

Add water to the pressure cooker according to the
manufacturer's instructions. Put a layer of greens in
the steamer insert. Mix the spices and garlic with some
salt and pepper. Put a little of the mixture on the
greens, then add more greens. Add another sprinkling
of spices and garlic. Continue this way until all the
greens and seasonings are in the pot.

Clamp on the lid, bring to full pressure, and cook for
2 minutes. Release pressure immediately if you want
the greens to retain a good bit of bite. If you want
them lusciously soft, leave it to vent gradually. Plonk
everything into a large serving bowl and toss with the
butter. The juice of half a lemon will complete the
picture, though it isn't essential.

braised cabbage

Meltingly soft braised cabbage has a way of winning over even those who say they don't like cabbage. With conventional methods it takes anything upwards of 45 minutes. In the pressure cooker, you need to apply heat for all of 10 minutes. This method works equally well with white, red and Savoy cabbage. If using red, put some red wine vinegar or red wine in with the stock. The bacon is optional, but I urge you to use it.

Serves 4–6 as a side dish

3 tablespoons extra virgin olive oil, duck or goose fat, or a couple of good knobs of butter
4–5 rashers of thickly-cut streaky bacon or pancetta
1 large cabbage (around 1kg), trimmed, cored and sliced as thickly as you like
seasonings of choice: dried herbs, whole or powdered spices
2 garlic cloves, finely chopped
300ml chicken or meat stock
salt and freshly ground black pepper

Put the oil, fat or butter in the pressure cooker. Use a pair of kitchen scissors to snip the bacon into the pot, aiming for thick shreds (lardons). Heat gently until the bacon starts to sizzle and colour lightly, around 3–5 minutes, then put in all the remaining ingredients.

Season with salt and pepper (easy on the salt), and toss thoroughly. Clamp on the lid, bring to full pressure and cook for 5 minutes. Release pressure immediately if you want the cabbage to retain a bit of bite. If you want it lusciously soft, leave it to vent gradually.

braised
red
cabbage

This needs slightly different treatment for aesthetic as well as gastronomic reasons.

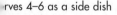

Serves 4–6 as a side dish

large red cabbage, cored, halved
and thickly sliced
medium red onion,
coarsely chopped
garlic cloves, finely chopped
4 tablespoons duck or goose fat
3 juniper berries
teaspoon dill seeds
teaspoon caraway seeds
teaspoon fennel seeds
teaspoons sugar or honey
0ml good chicken stock
ml red wine vinegar
ml dry red wine

Put the cabbage, onion, garlic and fat in the pressure cooker. Toss well over a medium heat for a minute or two, just to spread the fat around evenly. Add the remaining ingredients, clamp on the lid and bring up to full pressure. Cook for 5 minutes.

At this point, the cabbage will be soft but with a good hint of bite. If you like it that way, release the pressure immediately. If you leave it to vent gradually, the cabbage will be very soft. Your decision!

brussels sprouts with shallots

he secret of this dish is a really good stock. If you haven't got any,
ake something else.

tablespoons extra virgin olive oil,
 vegetable oil or duck fat
-4 shallots, finely chopped
00g Brussels sprouts, base trimmed
 and outer leaves removed if dry
 or mottled with yellow
00ml rich chicken, duck
 or beef stock
tablespoon cider vinegar
lt and freshly ground black pepper

Heat the fat in the pressure cooker and gently cook
the shallots just to get them smelling good, around
1 minute.

Mix in the sprouts, then pour in the stock and vinegar
and season well with salt and pepper. Clamp on the
lid, bring to full pressure and cook for 2 minutes.
Release pressure immediately.

pulses

Once you've cooked pulses in a pressure cooker, you'll never use any other method. Cooking times in an open pot range from 45 minutes to 2 hours. The pressure cooker cuts this to 10 minutes or less, and cooks them to a much better consistency. A real no-brainer. If they're not done when you pop the lid off, just put it back on and give them a few minutes more. Even with the extra cooking, you're still using much less energy than you would with open-pan cooking. NB: in all cases, you should turn the heat off and leave the pressure to return to normal by slow release. The extra time completes cooking without extra energy use.

timing pulses

There are many variables when cooking pulses, but I've found that all of them cook in roughly the same time:

Larger whole pulses (e.g. cannellini beans, chickpeas, kidney beans)
9–10 minutes for soft
6–7 minutes for al dente

Hulled pulses (e.g. red lentils)
4–5 minutes

Small whole pulses (e.g. Puy lentils)
5–6 minutes

Your preference will depend on what the pulses are for. If they will be cooked again, or if they're for a salad, al dente is good. If you want them soft and mushy, so you get some of the internal starch coming out to thicken the liquid, then the longer time is probably right.

basic braised beans

you're making beans in the pressure cooker, you can just cook them in
water or stock until soft. For just a very little extra effort, however, you can add
flavour to them at the first stage. This will make it easier, and more tasty, to use
them in any of the recipes (see pages 174–176) for reused beans. Use duck
fat, bacon fat, vegetable oil or olive oil. And while the stock should be
homemade if possible, don't fret if you have to use cubes.

00g white or cannellini beans,
  soaked overnight
medium carrots, finely chopped
small leek, white part only, finely
  chopped
sticks of celery, finely chopped
garlic cloves, finely chopped
tablespoons oil or fat
teaspoon herbes de Provence
large bay leaf
round 1 litre stock

Drain the beans. Put all ingredients except the beans and
the stock into the pressure cooker, and sweat them (cook
them gently without colouring) for 3–4 minutes, stirring a
few times. When they are smelling very fragrant, mix in
the beans. Pour in the stock, making sure there is enough
to cover the beans by around 2.5cm. But remember:
don't fill the pot by more than two thirds or three quarters,
depending on the manufacturer's instructions. Clamp on
the lid, bring to full pressure, and cook for 8 minutes if
you're eating the beans immediately, 6 minutes if they will
be cooked in another dish, venting the steam gradually.

poultry and meat

chicken with limes and spicy tomato sauce

This is a great dish for an informal dinner party. Serve with rice or mashed potatoes to soak up the flavourful cooking liquid.

Serves 4

8 chicken pieces, thighs and/or
   drumsticks as preferred
a little vegetable oil
2 medium onions, coarsely chopped
1–2 small green chillies, deseeded
   if you wish
pinch of dried oregano
2 teaspoons flour
4 limes, preferably unwaxed, halved
16–24 cloves of garlic, peeled
   but left whole
400g tin of tomatoes
150ml dry white wine or
   chicken stock
parsley or fresh coriander for
   garnish, finely chopped

Heat enough vegetable oil in the pressure cooker or in a frying pan (already used for vegetables, if possible) to coat the bottom. Brown the chicken in batches, trying to get some colour on all surfaces; don't despair if you can't brown them evenly. When they're all done, add a little more oil if needed and cook the onions briefly to get some colour into them – just a couple of minutes will do. Stir in the chillies, oregano, flour, lime halves and garlic, and finally the tomatoes and liquid.

Put the chicken on top, season with salt and pepper, and clamp the lid on. Bring up to full pressure and cook for 10 minutes, then turn the heat off and let the steam vent gradually. Garnish with the herbs, and serve with rice or mashed potatoes to soak up the flavourful cooking liquid.

chicken, squash, turnips and spices

A one-pot meal for 4 people. If you don't have access to turnips, parsnips will do just as well.

chicken pieces, breast or
  preferably leg, separated into
  thighs and drumsticks
round 125ml vegetable oil
small turnips, scrubbed well
  but unpeeled
small butternut squash, quartered,
  deseeded and peeled (optional)
lemons, halved
cinnamon stick
teaspoon each of cumin and
  coriander seeds
salt and freshly ground black pepper
00ml chicken stock, dry white wine
  or water (or a combination)

Put the chicken pieces in the pot two at a time with the vegetable oil, and brown very quickly. Take them out and put in the turnips, then the squash, then the lemons and then the spices. Put the chicken pieces on top and season with salt and pepper, then pour on whichever liquid you are using. Bring up to full pressure and cook for 10 minutes. Release pressure immediately and serve as soon as you can open the lid.

Plain boiled rice makes a good accompaniment, and some chopped parsley on top adds a little colour.

thai curry, red or green

This recipe is heavily adapted from a pair in Kelly Simon's *Thai Cooking*, part of Little, Brown's excellent 'Foods of the World' series. Both will be much better if you use homemade curry paste. But they're delicious with a good version from a jar. Feeds 4 with some leftovers (and the leftovers are good).

4 chicken legs or breasts
vegetable oil
3 tablespoons Thai curry paste,
  red or green
2–3 plump garlic cloves,
  finely chopped
1–3 small chillies, finely chopped
1 lemongrass stalk, cut into
  2.5cm lengths
2 tablespoons Thai fish sauce
1 small tin of coconut cream
300ml chicken stock
4–5 kaffir lime leaves, soaked
  in warm water if dried
mint, Thai basil or coriander leaves,
  to finish

Skin the chicken if you wish. Divide the chicken legs into thighs and drumsticks, or cut the breasts in half. Put enough oil in the pressure cooker to film the bottom generously, then brown the chicken lightly; you'll have to do this in three or four batches. Remove the browned pieces to a plate.

Spoon out all but around 1 tablespoon of vegetable oil from the cooker and add the curry paste. Cook over a low heat for a few seconds, then add the garlic, chillies and lemongrass. Stir for a few moments, just to get the garlic smelling fragrant, then put the chicken back in and toss to coat it in the curry mixture. Add the fish sauce, coconut cream and stock. Stir well and clamp the lid on. Bring to full pressure and cook for 10 minutes, then turn off the heat and leave for 5 minutes. Release the steam and serve immediately with lots of leaves to scatter on top, plus a big pot of plain rice.

guinea fowl
with cider and spices

Guinea fowl should have a rich, slightly gamey flavour that takes very well
to the type of treatment you would usually use for pheasant. The bird can
be browned in the pressure cooker but it's easier in a frying pan. If possible,
use one that you've already used (or plan to use) for cooking lidded
vegetables as a side dish.

Serves 2 generously,
** or 4 with plenty of side dishes**

1 guinea fowl
vegetable oil
1 large onion, thickly sliced
2 whole cloves
1 cinnamon stick
2 allspice berries
2 juniper berries
2 tablespoons plain flour
450ml dry or medium-dry cider
salt and freshly ground black pepper

Brown the bird lightly in just enough oil to cover the
bottom of a heavy pan (or the pressure cooker if you
wish). You can't brown every single bit of it, but doing
both breasts and the back will suffice. Remove the bird
and put the onion in the bottom of the pressure cooker
followed by the spices and the flour, distributing both well
over the onions. Place the bird on top, add the cider and
season with salt and pepper.

Clamp the lid on and bring up to full pressure, then
cook for 15 minutes if you like poultry à point (just done),
20 minutes if you like it closer to the falling-off-the-bone
stage. Leave to vent the steam gradually, then serve
immediately with rice or potatoes.

beans and a bone

nearly every cuisine where meat is eaten, there is at least one recipe that
combines a big hunk of meat on an even bigger length of bone with a potful
beans. This kind of dish is a way of feeding hungry people the flavour of
eat without having to spend too much money, and it might have been
ade with the pressure cooker in mind. Here is a specimen recipe, using
hichever meat takes your fancy. My list of candidates would include the
llowing options (choosing just one from the list): 1 pig's trotter or lamb
ank; 1 smoked pork knuckle (2 if they are very small); 1 knuckle of cooked
am, soaked if it is very salty.

erves 4

ortion of meat per person
see preamble)
0g kidney beans, soaked overnight
t and freshly ground black pepper
getable oil, butter, bacon fat
or duck fat
arge onion, thickly sliced
ead of garlic, cloves separated
ut unpeeled
ticks of celery, cut lengthwise
nto 2–3 pieces
arrots, cut lengthwise into
2–3 pieces
easpoon paprika, cayenne
or chilli powder
0ml beef, chicken or
egetable stock
0g tin good-quality plum tomatoes
t and freshly ground black pepper

Cook the kidney beans in the pressure cooker with 1 litre
water for 5 minutes. Vent the steam immediately and
drain the beans. Wipe out the pressure cooker and add
enough oil, butter or fat to film the bottom generously.
Cook the onion over a moderate heat for a few minutes,
just long enough to soften slightly and get a little colour
into it, around 5 minutes. Mix in all the remaining
ingredients, add the kidney beans and put the meat on
top. Season with a little salt and plenty of pepper.

Clamp the lid on, bring to full pressure, and cook for
35 minutes. Vent the steam gradually. The meat should
be just about falling off the bone, but not completely
dried out. Note: any leftover liquid will make a
memorable addition to soup or a rustic sauce.

lamb shanks with apricots

This is based on an Iraqi dish called *hamuth heloo*, which I read about in *The Complete Middle East Cookbook* by Tess Mallos. My version simplifies the original, which calls for a combination of dried fruits; it also uses lamb shanks, which are exceptionally well suited to the pressure cooker, rather than chunks of lamb. Really tasty stuff.

Serves 4

4 lamb shanks, or 2 or 3 if
   they are very large
vegetable oil
1 large onion, coarsely chopped
a piece of cinnamon
1 lemon, halved, plus another
   for its zest
250g dried apricots
3 teaspoons brown sugar
200ml water or chicken stock

Pour oil into the pressure cooker to film the bottom generously, then turn the heat on medium-high and brown the lamb as evenly as you can. Remove to a plate and put the onion in the pressure cooker. Brown it lightly, then put the lamb back in the pot with the cinnamon, lemon, apricots and sugar.

Pour in the water, or chicken stock. Clamp the lid on, bring up to full pressure and cook for 25 minutes. Turn the heat off and let the steam vent gradually. In the meantime, grate the zest from the second lemon.

Cut the meat off the bone if you aren't serving one shank per person. Degrease the cooking juices and serve each diner with lamb, some juice and a good sprinkling of lemon zest. Plain rice is the natural side dish, but a slice of good crusty bread would suffice.

pork, potatoes and crackling

is recipe, if I may say so, is a humdinger.
e pressure cooker does not produce
ackling from pork rind, but it does produce
ork rind that's all set for crackling when
posed to the high, dry heat of a frying
an. So, this a two-step procedure. A piece
boned and rolled shoulder of pork is the
o choice here. Note that the recipe makes
o many potatoes for 2 people, but the leftovers will be delicious either
heated or turned into a stewy, curry-ish concoction. And also note: while
e pork is getting pressured, you should cook a green vegetable in the
ing pan you'll be using to brown the meat.

ves 2

Og large new potatoes
mall onions, sliced
arrots, sliced or cut into
hick batons
Oml light stock or water
easpoon dried herbs – herbes de
rovence, dried thyme, rosemary
or sage
t and freshly ground black pepper
50g piece of boned and rolled
ork, around 10cm long and
Ocm thick
etable oil

Put the potatoes in the pot, followed by the onions, carrots,
stock or water (there should be just enough liquid barely to
cover the vegetables) and herbs. Season with salt and
plenty of pepper. Put the pork on top and clamp on the lid.
Bring to full pressure, then turn down the heat and cook
for 10 minutes. Vent the steam immediately when the timer
goes off.

Film a heavy frying pan generously with oil; the pan must
be large enough to accommodate the meat. Put it over a
medium heat and lift the pork out of the pressure cooker
with a long pair of tongs. When the oil is hot, put the pork
in the pan skin-side down and cook for 4–5 minutes, long
enough to turn the skin to crackling; if it isn't lying flat, turn
it to crackle as much of the skin as possible. To finish,
brown the meaty surfaces lightly. The whole procedure
should take no more than 10 minutes – which, added to
the pressure cooking time, is far less than you would need
if you were roasting the joint.

Serve with the potatoes and some of the cooking liquid
as gravy.

short ribs with beer and spices

Short ribs begin life as long ribs: they're the long, straight bones sawn off a rib of beef when it's prepared for roasting or cutting up for steaks. They have relatively little meat on them, but the meat is exceedingly tasty, and the cut is cheap. Get the butcher to cut the ribs into pieces around 10cm long. And if they're very fatty, trim off most of the fat but not all – leaving a little on makes the dish more succulent. If you're cooking a vegetable in a lidded frying pan which can be served at room temperature, you can cook them first and then reuse the same pan (without washing) for browning the beef.

Serves 4

vegetable oil
4 short ribs (around 2kg), cut into
  10cm pieces
1 large onion, sliced
3–4 garlic cloves
1 teaspoon each of ground cumin,
  coriander and cinnamon
2 cloves
1 allspice berry
1 tablespoon plain flour
a 660ml bottle of any beer,
  but not lager

Heat enough vegetable oil in the pressure cooker or in a frying pan to cover the base. Brown the ribs a few pieces at a time, trying to get some colour on all surfaces; don't despair if you can't brown them evenly. When they're all done, add a little more oil if needed and cook the onion slices briefly to get some colour into them – just a couple of minutes will do.

Return the browned ribs with the remaining ingredients to the pressure cooker and clamp the lid on. Bring up to full pressure and cook for 25 minutes, then turn the heat off and let the steam vent gradually. As soon as you can remove the lid, test the beef for doneness by pulling off a bit and eating it. If it isn't meltingly soft, put it back in and cook for another 5 minutes. Serve with rice or mashed potatoes to soak up the flavourful cooking liquid.

It's a good idea to test just about anything you've cooked in the pressure cooker as soon as the lid can be released. If the dish isn't done, you can just clamp the lid back on, bring it up to full pressure and finish off cooking. For reheating, however, it's best not to use pressure: too much danger of overcooking.

curried beef

is is even better when reheated. If you can get your hands on shin of beef, at is an ideal cut to use instead of braising steak.

erves 6–8

slabs of good braising steak,
around 4cm thick
ound 3 tablespoons flour
lt and freshly ground black pepper
tablespoons vegetable oil
large carrots, cut into 5cm lengths
large onion, cut into large chunks
garlic cloves, peeled and halved
-2 tablespoons mild curry powder
0g tin good-quality plum tomatoes
od beef stock as needed
d wine as needed

Dust the beef with the flour, season with salt and pepper and heat the oil to medium-hot in the pressure cooker.

Brown the meat lightly, no more than two pieces at a time.

Remove to a plate or bowl as they're done. When they're all done, add the carrots, onion, garlic and curry powder to the pressure cooker. Stir for a minute, adding a little water to deglaze. Return the meat to the pressure cooker and add the tomatoes, stock and wine. There should be just enough liquid to cover the meat; try to use around half wine and half stock. Clamp the lid on, bring to full pressure and cook for 30 minutes. Release pressure immediately and check the meat; it should be soft, and tender when poked with a fork or – my preferred utensil – a chopstick. Cook again for 5 more minutes if you think it needs it. Serve with mashed potatoes or plain rice.

beef stew with chickpeas and lemon

This is based on an Iranian dish which I was told about by the owners of The Pure Meat Company – my local butcher, fishmonger and place of worship. From starting the chickpeas to revealing the rich, warming stew, ready to eat, the cooking takes under an hour – ideal for a hasty dinner party.

Serves 4

350g dried chickpeas
vegetable oil
4 slices of good braising steak, 4cm thick and around 200–250g each
1–2 fairly large onions, thinly sliced
4–6 garlic cloves, coarsely chopped
300ml flavourful liquid – stock, wine, or a combination
400g tin good-quality plum tomatoes
½ teaspoon each of ground cinnamon and turmeric
a pinch of allspice
1 lemon, quartered

Soak the chickpeas overnight and drain well. Cook them in the pressure cooker with 1 litre water for 5 minutes. Vent the steam immediately and drain. Wipe out the pressure cooker and add enough oil to film the bottom generously. Put it over a medium-high heat and quickly brown the beef on both sides; you will have to do this in 2 or even 4 batches. Remove each browned piece to the bowl with the chickpeas. When they're all done, add the onions and garlic and brown very lightly (no more than 1 minute), then pour in the liquid. Add the tomatoes and seasonings.

Return the chickpeas and beef to the pressure cooker, with the chickpeas on the bottom and the beef sitting on top of them. Put the lemon quarters on top, clamp on the lid and bring up to full pressure. Cook for 25 minutes, then turn off the heat and vent gradually.

rice

You can pressure-cook plain rice, but I'm not completely convinced of its advantages. Cooking rice in the regular way doesn't use a lot of water. Or energy, since it's done with the magic lid on top of the pot. If you want to give it a go, however, here is the formula:

• Use washed rice for less sticky results.

• Put the rice in the pot with double the volume of water or stock.

• Cook for 5 minutes.

• Release the steam immediately.

Risotto is an entirely different matter. When cooked conventionally, it takes a long time – and a lot of effort on the cook's part. While saving your own energy doesn't qualify as green cooking, the shortened cooking time certainly does. So does the elimination of a second saucepan for heating the stock.

basic risotto

Serves 2, or 3–4 as a side dish

1 small onion, finely chopped
a good knob of butter,
    or a smaller knob with
    1 tablespoon extra virgin olive oil
300ml Arborio rice
600ml chicken stock
salt and freshly ground black pepper
a small handful of fresh parsley,
    finely chopped
freshly grated Parmesan

Put the onion and butter in the pressure cooker and cook over a gentle heat. Sweat the onion (gently cook it without colouring it) for a few minutes, just to soften it slightly and take away the raw flavour. Add the rice and stir it into the onions to coat it well and get a sheen of translucence in the grains. This will take 2–3 minutes.

Now add the stock, a little salt and a lot of pepper. Bring up to full pressure and cook for 5 minutes. Vent the steam immediately and remove the lid as soon as possible. Stir in the chopped parsley and a little Parmesan and leave, with the lid slightly off, to finish cooking for 2–3 minutes. Everyone can add extra Parmesan as they see fit.

congee

congee is a Chinese creation (often eaten for breakfast) which comes very close to winning the title of Ultimate Comfort Food. It's often translated as 'rice gruel', which makes it sound like something from Oliver Twist. It isn't. It's great. And best cooked in the pressure cooker. Here is a basic recipe and a few variations.

serves 3–4 as a lunch dish

50g long-grain rice
5 litres water or light chicken stock
(a single stock cube is fine for this
quantity of water)
piece of lean stewing beef,
200–300g
2 cloves garlic, finely chopped
medium onion, coarsely chopped
small piece of ginger, peeled
and finely chopped

If you wish, you can soak the rice before cooking. This removes some of the surface starch and gives the congee a thinner, less gloopy consistency than unwashed rice, which yields more thickness and stickiness. It's a matter of taste; I suggest trying it both ways to see which you prefer. To soak the rice, just cover well with water and stir it by hand for a couple of minutes. Drain the rice and put in the pressure cooker with all the remaining ingredients. Clamp the lid on, bring to full pressure and cook for 20 minutes. It will be done at that point, so you can release the pressure immediately, but it can also sit with the heat turned off for slow release.

Pull the meat out of the congee; it should be perfectly soft. Cut it into thin shreds or dice, return to the pot and stir in. Serve very hot, with soy sauce, sesame oil and (inauthentic) Thai or Vietnamese fish sauce as condiments. Some chopped fresh coriander adds colour and extra flavour, and chopped chilli or chilli sauce add fire. If you're having it for breakfast, however, I'd serve it just on its own.

variations

pork congee
use a piece of pork shoulder instead of beef. If very fatty, trim the fat but leave on any skin; this adds texture and body to the congee.

chicken congee
use frozen chicken pieces, leg for preference, instead of beef. They must be frozen or they'll cook to nothingness – and even from frozen they will end up very well cooked.

vegetarian congee
Cook without any meat, and release pressure immediately the 20 minutes are up. While the congee is cooking, dice 1 large carrot and 2 stalks of celery. Add them to the cooked congee along with a large handful of frozen peas. Clamp the lid back on and bring to full pressure, then cook for another 2 minutes. Vent immediately.

potted dishes

If you have a large enough pressure cooker, you can put another vessel inside it and cook a range of dishes to excellent effect. These are things that wouldn't cook properly without a separate container, because they'd catch on the bottom of the pot, or which would be difficult to serve.

You just have to watch for a few points when cooking in a pot:

• Use a vessel that's small enough to allow steam to circulate freely; there should be at least 2.5cm on all sides.

• Fill the pressure cooker with water to a depth that barely grazes the bottom of the steamer insert.

• Don't over-fill the cooking vessel. Leave a space of around 1.5cm between the top of the food and the rim of the dish.

• Take care when removing the vessel from the pressure cooker, as it will still be hot. Don't tip it, as there may be liquid inside.

See opposite for an example of the genre.

a rustic terrine

is is a very straightforward country-style terrine, but the method can be adapted more glamorous versions. Get your butcher to mince the pork using the coarse medium plate on the mincer – or mince it yourself using a food processor, but ke care not to over-process. Note: these measurements are to fit comfortably in soufflé dish 16cm in diameter and 9cm high.

ves 6–8 as a starter

g (around one thin slice)
of good white bread
gg
easpoon dried mixed herbs,
uch as herbes de Provence
inch of ground allspice
4 garlic cloves, finely chopped
3 slices of onion, finely chopped
mall handful of parsley,
oarsely chopped
ml dry white wine
and freshly ground black pepper
g minced fatty pork (see above)

Chop the bread into small pieces and put it in a mixing bowl along with all other ingredients except the pork. Season well with salt and pepper, then mix thoroughly, breaking up the bread into a mush. Add the pork and blend well – your hands are the best tool for this.

Pack the mixture into the soufflé dish, pressing firmly but not squashing all the air out. Smooth the top, or leave a rough texture by running the back of a fork over it. Put the steamer insert in your pressure cooker and fill with water to the bottom of the insert. Put in the dish, clamp the lid on and cook for 20 minutes once full pressure has been reached.

Vent the steam immediately and remove the lid as soon as you can. Test the terrine by pressing down on the middle. It should feel only very slightly soft, or completely firm. If it's too soft, put the lid back on and cook for another 5 minutes, again with immediate venting.

Put a small plate on top of the terrine and weight down the plate with something heavy – a large tin is ideal. Leave to cool to room temperature, then refrigerate overnight.

This terrine does not look lovely on top because it doesn't get brown. To spruce up the colour, you can scatter it with chopped herbs before serving. And take it out of the fridge at least an hour before serving, to show off the flavour to its full potential.

double-cooked dishes

Meat and poultry take longer to cook in the pressure cooker than vegetables. If you put them all in at the same time, the vegetables will be cooked to mush by the time the meat is finished. The solution: cooking in stages. First you cook the meat, then vent the steam immediately and add the vegetables. Used in this way, any of the hearty meat dishes above can have vegetables added for a final few minutes of cooking and turn into a one-dish meal.

I suggest that you master the basics of pressure cooking before you try using the double-cooked method.

Once you've got the hang of it, however, it's a simple enough process.

For a purpose-built example of double cooking, here's a recipe to try. But there are dozens of dishes that can be adapted to the method – just about any dish where meat or poultry and vegetables are combined. Again, think about your favourite recipes and how they can be modified for speedy-quick pressure cooking.

chicken with 40 cloves of garlic

This is adapted from one of the all-time great chicken dishes, and perfectly suited to cooking in the pressure cooker. Don't be frightened by the prodigious quantity of garlic – cooked in this way, those fragrant bulbs lose much of their pungency and won't contaminate your breath the next day.

Serves 4

around 150ml extra virgin olive oil
a whole chicken that will fit in your pressure cooker
50ml dry white wine
salt and freshly ground black pepper
4 heads of garlic, separated into cloves but unpeeled

Put enough oil in the pressure cooker to film the bottom generously and put over a medium-hot heat. Brown the breast of the chicken lightly, turning to get both sides a little colour – but don't worry about even browning. Turn it over and brown briefly on the back. Now add the wine and a very good dose of salt and pepper.

Clamp the lid on, bring up to full pressure and cook for 10 minutes. Vent the steam immediately and open the pot as soon as you're able to, then pour in the remainder of the oil and all the garlic, making sure the cloves all land in the oil. Put the lid back on, bring up to full pressure and cook for 10 minutes. Release the steam immediately and leave to rest for 5 minutes before carving.

Serve the chicken on a platter with the garlic cloves strewn about; some chopped parsley adds a bit of colour. Pour the liquid into a warmed jug and encourage your guests to splash plenty over their chicken, for mopping up with crusty bread or white rice.

5.no-cook cooking

It's hardly worth pointing out that the best way to save energy in cooking is not to use any heat at all: in other words, to serve the food raw. The range of wonderful dishes made with no heat is limited but a handful of uncooked dishes rank high in the gastronomic pantheon, and some of those are given here.

picy gazpacho
vith sherry vinegar

is is based on an idea from my brother Henry, an excellent cook. The chillies
me from him, and if you like very spicy food, leave the seeds in. The sherry
egar is from me. Both items can be omitted, but the soup is much more
citing if they're in there.

ves 4–6

 red, ripe tomatoes
 arlic cloves
 ild green chilli, deseeded
 and freshly ground
 lack pepper
 ablespoons extra virgin olive oil
 0cm length of cucumber
 mall onion
 reen pepper
 ices of good white bread
 ml sherry vinegar

Core the tomatoes, remove the seeds and jelly from
a quarter of them and reserve. Coarsely chop the
remaining tomatoes with the garlic and chilli. Purée the
mixture in a blender, then strain and season well with
salt and pepper. Stir in the oil, cover and refrigerate
for at least 1 hour.

Peel the cucumber, halve it lengthwise and scoop out
the seeds. Chop the reserved tomatoes, cucumber,
onion and peppers into fine dice. Dice the bread as
fine as you can get it and put all these garnishes into
separate serving bowls. Refrigerate until needed.

When you're ready to serve, taste the purée: if it tastes
too strongly of tomato, thin it out with water or chicken
stock. Add more salt and pepper as needed. Stir in the
sherry vinegar and serve immediately with the garnishes
passed separately.

fennel salad
with mustard vinaigrette

If you slice the fennel thin enough, this can be ready to eat in 15 minutes.
If the slices are thicker, extra time in the fridge will soften them further – which
is a good thing, in my view.

Serves 4

2–3 small bulbs of fennel
  (about 500g)
1 tablespoon red wine vinegar
fine salt
1 small red onion, thinly sliced
2 tablespoons extra virgin olive oil
½ teaspoon Dijon mustard
juice of ½ small lemon
black pepper

Top and tail the fennel bulbs, and cut out the cores if
you wish. Then slice them as thin as you can. If you can
manage paper-thin slices (easiest using a mandolin),
they will soften and soak up the vinegar within minutes.
Thicker slices (around the thickness of a £1 coin, for
instance), may take an hour or two. Whatever the
thickness, put the slices in a bowl with the vinegar and
sprinkle with a generous pinch of fine salt. Add the
onion slices. Toss well and leave while you finish the
rest of the vinaigrette.

Whisk the oil, mustard and lemon juice with a very
generous dose of black pepper. If you prefer, you can
put them in a small jar and shake vigorously. Pour over
the fennel and mix well, then leave for 10–15 minutes
before eating – or longer if you want your fennel to lose
all its crunch.

panzanella

The great 'bread salad' of Tuscany was devised, or so it's assumed, as a way of using day-old bread. What started out of necessity, like so many other instances of peasant frugality, has ended up being a delicacy. If the bread isn't stale, just toss with the other ingredients and leave to soften a little before serving. This version is not entirely authentic, but varying ingredients is one of the pleasures of the dish.

Serves 4 as a summer lunch

thick slices of good white bread,
or around ½ a baguette
large, ripe tomatoes, cored
and cut into small chunks
red and/or yellow peppers,
deseeded and cut into
small chunks
large cucumber, deseeded and
cut into small chunks

The dressing
plump clove of garlic,
very finely chopped
-3 anchovy fillets, drained
and very finely chopped
teaspoon capers, drained and
very finely chopped
0ml extra virgin olive oil
tablespoon red wine vinegar
lack pepper

Tear the bread into rough chunks. If it is old, sprinkle the chunks generously with cold water and leave them to soften for 15 minutes while you prepare the other ingredients. Squeeze the water out until the bread is soft and fairly dry.

Combine the other salad ingredients in a bowl.

To make the dressing, combine all the ingredients in a small bowl. Whisk thoroughly with a generous grinding of black pepper but no salt – the capers and anchovies are already salty.

Dress the salad, toss well, and leave for 15–30 minutes before serving.

spicy stuffed tomato

A great summer dish when there are good ripe tomatoes around; this is sort of like a solid gazpacho. Serves 1 as a starter or a light lunch dish.

1 large, ripe tomato
a 5cm length of cucumber
1 anchovy fillet, finely chopped
4–5 sprigs of fresh coriander,
  roughly chopped
around ½ teaspoon finely
  chopped, deseeded green chilli
1 small spring onion,
  finely chopped
½ teaspoon wine or cider vinegar
½ teaspoon extra virgin olive oil
salt and freshly ground
  black pepper

Cut the top off the tomato and scoop out as much of the flesh as possible using a small, sharp knife (a serrated blade makes it easier) and a teaspoon. Save the tomato innards for stock or soup.

Peel the cucumber if you wish, halve it lengthwise and scoop out the seeds. Chop into fine dice, mix with the remaining ingredients, seasoning with a little salt and a lot of pepper. Pack the mixture into the tomato and eat within 30 minutes.

courgette salad with prosciutto

The key to success is slicing the courgettes as near as you can get to paper-thin, and the best way to do it is on a mandolin. Instead of prosciutto you can use smoked fish such as trout or haddock. Serves 4.

4 smallish courgettes, around
  15cm in length, sliced on the
  bias as thin as possible
around 60ml of vinaigrette
black pepper
4 paper-thin slices of the best
  prosciutto (or jamón Serrano)
  you can find
10–12 chives, snipped or chopped
  into tiny pieces
extra virgin olive oil

Lay the courgettes on 4 serving plates in overlapping layers. Brush them with the vinaigrette, making sure that they're fully coated; you don't need a lot of dressing, but you do need to cover the slices fully. Grind on some black pepper, and leave for 30 minutes or so, to let the dressing soften up the courgettes.

To serve, either tear the ham in rough pieces or just leave in slices. Put the ham on top of the courgettes and sprinkle on the chives. Add a few more drops of oil and serve immediately.

cabbage with vinegar and garlic

I've been making this stuff for years after seeing a recipe like it in Craig Claiborne and Virginia Lee's *The Chinese Cookbook*. It's so popular with everyone that I really ought to keep a dish on hand at all times – and you should consider doing the same.

Serves 4–6 as a nibble with drinks or as a side dish

500g white cabbage
2–3 tablespoons red wine vinegar
fine salt
2 large garlic cloves, peeled and smashed
a small knob of fresh ginger, peeled and thinly sliced
1 small chilli, de-stemmed and halved lengthwise

Trim the cabbage of any dried out leaves, cut a slice off the base and cut out the core. Halve the cabbage lengthwise, then slice it as thinly as you can – the thinner it is, the sooner it will be ready. Put the shreds in a non-reactive dish (glass, plastic or stainless steel), and toss with the vinegar plus a generous dose of salt.

Toss the garlic, ginger and chilli thoroughly with the cabbage, cover and refrigerate.

The cabbage should be tossed and turned every day, or twice a day, to redistribute the vinegar. It can be eaten the next day, but over 3–4 days it will soften and lose more of the raw flavour. Especially good with pork or lamb.

cured salmon

...lmon sprinkled with salt, pepper and flavourings, then left to cure in the ...dge, is just as good as smoked salmon. The model here is gravlax, ...voured with fresh dill (and sugar traditionally but optionally). But you can ...e other flavourings, as long as you follow the same principle. The key to ...ccess lies in using the right amount of salt, not too much and not too little. ...e best way to measure is by surface area, not weight of fish. Since cured ...lmon is easy to make in small quantities, I have given a recipe that will ...rve four to six as a starter. If you're using a whole side or a larger piece, ...t get out a ruler and calculator – adjusting the quantities is simple work.

...piece of very fresh salmon fillet,
...skin left on, around 10 x 15cm
...teaspoons medium-coarse salt
...peppermill

...avourings:

...ravlax
...ely chop a small bunch of dill ...d press it onto the flesh once salt ...d pepper have been applied.

...iced salmon
...x ½ teaspoon each of powdered ...min and coriander into the salt ...xture, and sprinkle on the salmon ...in the main recipe.

...nnel salmon
...ast 1 teaspoon of fennel seeds by ...ating them in a small uncoated ...e. not non-stick) frying pan until ...grant. Scatter them over the fish ...er you grind on the pepper. If ...u're making this, serve it with the ...nel salad on page 140.

Pull out the fine 'pin bones' from the salmon using your fingers and a pair of clean tweezers. Put the fish in a shallow plastic dish and sprinkle the salt evenly over the whole surface. If you're unsure of how much to use, proceed very cautiously to cover the fish, then use up the rest in a second pass.

Now grind on the pepper, using a fairly coarse grind. Give it a light dusting for a mild pepper flavour and a heavy coating if you want the pepper to be more prominent. When the whole surface is covered, press the pepper gently into the fish using the ball of your thumb.

Now add flavourings of your choice if you wish, using the brief list on the left as a guideline. Press them into the flesh.

If you wish, you can now lay a sheet of clingfilm on top of the fish to protect it completely from the air. I just cover the dish with its lid and put it straight in the fridge. Keep it there for 2 days and it will be ready to eat. When ready to serve, take a very sharp, thin-bladed knife and slice on an angle to the work surface.

This is a light cure, so doesn't keep for much more than 3 days.

mackerel ceviche

Serves 2–4

4 small mackerel, filleted
juice of 2 lemons or 3 limes
1 medium onion, finely sliced
1 dried red chilli, crumbled
   (optional)
½ teaspoon cumin seeds
½ teaspoon coriander seeds
a handful of chopped fresh
   coriander
a few cracked black peppercorns

Trim the fish well and cut it into chunks or slices cut at an angle – or have the fishmonger do this for you. Put the pieces in a non-reactive bowl (glass, plastic or stainless steel) just large enough to hold them. Mix the marinade ingredients, pour the mixture over the fish and toss well.

Cover the dish and marinate in the fridge at least overnight, turning once or twice. One day of marinating will leave the fish with a hint of rawness at the centre, 2 days will make it fully firm. Before serving, drain the fish well. Serve with sliced tomatoes and toast or tortillas.

salted and marinated fish

This works best with smaller oily fish, especially anchovies, but also smaller herrings and sardines. The only fiddly bit is boning the fish – messy, time-consuming and frustrating if you're doing them in large quantities. But after that, it's the easiest thing in the world.

salting

Rub off any hard scales from the fish. Cut a small slit in the belly and work your thumbnail into the slit, gently pulling one fillet off the bone. Remove any traces of blood and put the fillet aside. Now work your nail under the backbone to pull the other fillet off. Repeat with all the fish.

Put a single layer of fillets in a flat-bottomed dish, skin side down, and add a light sprinkling of coarse salt. Put in another layer of fillets and salt again. Repeat until all the fillets are lightly coated.

Cover the dish and refrigerate for 24 hours. Rinse the fillets thoroughly under cold water and pat dry. Now you can proceed with marinating.

a simple marinade for salted fish

arts extra virgin olive oil
art lemon juice or
ed wine vinegar
arlic clove, coarsely chopped
w sprigs of parsley
w coriander seeds
nty of black pepper

Mix enough of the marinade to cover the fish completely. Pour it over, making sure that all the fleshy surfaces of the fillets have some contact with it.

Leave for 24–48 hours and eat with crusty bread or potato salad.

6. cooking for multiple meals

While you wouldn't get much joy out of eating a dish three nights in a row, there's a particular kind of pleasure that comes from discovering it in the freezer 6 weeks after you made it. You are spared the trouble of cooking that evening, almost as if someone else had come in to do it for you.

he rationale

There are three reasons for cooking this way.

Energy saving: most dishes use roughly the same amount of fuel regardless of the quantities you cook, and they can be reheated in the microwave or a saucepan in a matter of minutes. The energy savings with a microwave are greatest if the dish would ordinarily be oven-cooked, but there is a reduction even over cooking on the hob.

Water: if you cook the dish three separate times, you will have to wash up three cooking pots, three kitchen knives, three chopping boards and so forth. And needless to say, the water will have to be heated on each occasion, using more energy. With a dish from the freezer, the only thing needing washing is the container in which it was frozen.

But the best reason for multiple cooking is purely selfish: it saves you time. For a single effort, you get extra meals (two, three or even more) that you can pull out whenever you're ready to eat them. This is yet another example of green cooking as labour-saving cooking.

However, two warnings are required here:

n't make your life miserable (part 1)

This is important in every area of Green Kitchen practice, but perhaps nowhere as important as in planning multiple meals. For many people, and I am one of them, eating the same dish two days in a row becomes a chore rather than a pleasure; repeating over three or more days is a cause for resentment and outright rebellion. This is not what eating should be about.

If you are one of those people who can happily cook a dish and eat it every day for the next week, great. If you are not, then plan for longer storage of your multiply-cooked meals. Even I am not willing to sacrifice a varied diet for the sake of saving energy and water. You will go back to them a week or a month later. And you will do so with pleasure rather than resentment.

don't make your life miserable (part 2)

Life is hard, and busy. The last thing you want to do it is make it harder and busier. But you have to do that a little if you want to start making a habit of cooking for multiple meals. The operation requires thought and planning; it means trying to expand your brain-power to accommodate the shopping and cooking not just for one night but for two or more.

I know, from long personal experience, that it can be a bit of a burden. It's worth doing, however, for entirely selfish reasons along with the environmental reasons. If you prepare two meals in one go, you have another evening free – apart from reheating, which is the easiest form of cooking.

a word on food storage

All cooked food should be left to cool to room temperature and then put in a clean container, covered tightly, and stored in either the fridge or the freezer. In the fridge, it will last for a few days. In the freezer, it will last for a couple of months. Under no circumstances should food be left to sit at room temperature overnight. Never break this rule.

I will now tell you what I sometimes do with cooked food. I leave it in its cooking vessel overnight on the hob and then either re-cook it the following day or just heat it to full boiling for at least 5 minutes. Then I cool it, cover it and leave it again overnight. I do this mostly with stock, pulses and vegetable dishes, and sometimes with braised or pressure-cooked meat. I would never do it with anything containing fish. Neither I nor anyone in my family has ever fallen ill from this practice. It is possible that we all have very robust immune systems which protect us; it is also possible that we have robust immune systems because I do this. But you should never, ever follow my example, which breaks just about every rule of food safety.

freezing

This type of cooking would be impossible, or at least much more limited in scope, without a freezer. You have to be able to store the food in the freezer if you are not going to be eating it within a few days. See page 25 for advice on buying, using and maintaining freezer containers – essential pieces of kitchen hardware.

Not all dishes take well to freezing. You have to know what to cook – and what not to cook.

• As a general rule, the no-go list is populated by foods that are cooked either in completely 'dry' conditions or in a very little oil.
• Thus, roasted, grilled and fried or sautéed meats are the worst choices: their texture will suffer from freezing.
• Fully cooked vegetables are also inadvisable, because their texture too will be unacceptable once they're fully cooked. (Note, however, that they can be used in soups or stews on their emergence from the freezer because mushiness isn't a problem in those dishes.)

• The same applies to most pasta dishes unless they're baked items such as lasagne.

What does that leave you with? Plenty:

• Just about any food that's been cooked in wet conditions will freeze well. That includes soups, stews, pulses, sauces.
• Long-cooked meats also freeze well, as long as the surface is protected by liquid.
• I also like to prepare and cook large quantities of basic ingredients which get used in different forms in different types of dish; some of my favourites are described on the following pages.

approaches to multiple cooking

When I cook multiply, the effort takes one of three forms:

- Single ingredients
- Mixtures and sauces
- Whole dishes

I can't tell you which one you should aim for, because I don't know how you cook or what you like eating. I'll describe each of those options with a few examples, and let you ponder the question of what suits you and your target eatership. Multiple cooking is a way of thinking, not a set of hard-and-fast rules. Each home cook adapts it to suit his or her own needs and appetites.

single ingredients

The simplest way of making extra is making more of one of the things you're eating for dinner. In my kitchen, this usually means simple starch dishes or vegetables. They can be stored in the fridge or in the freezer, but I usually use the fridge because I manage to find ways of using the stuff pretty quickly. Among the items I make in excess:

- Any simply cooked vegetable, for use in soups or salads
- Bacon, for adding to simple meat, fish or poultry – and to salads and vegetables
- Poached or braised meat or feathered game
- Stock
- Pizza and bread dough
- Any starch except for pasta

favourite items of excess 1: potatoes

Any simple version of boiled, steamed or pressure-cooked potatoes can be made in excessive quantities for later reuse. Even baked potatoes are worth cooking in extra quantities, maximising oven usage, and storing in the fridge; sliced and fried in olive oil they are delicious. If boiled or steamed, floury potatoes such as main-crop King Edwards often acquire a tired, stale flavour after spending much more than a day in the fridge, but waxy potatoes, most new potatoes and Cyprus potatoes don't suffer at all; on the contrary, they firm up and become easier to handle when being sliced or broken up for further cooking. I have friends who disagree, but to my palate plainly cooked leftover new potatoes can serve honourably in various guises up to three or four days after the initial cooking. Store them airtight in the fridge, and follow these hints.

lidded new potatoes

Follow the recipe on page 59 but cook the (already-cooked) potatoes without water just long enough to heat through and crisp the skin a little, around 5 minutes.

potato salad

Follow your usual recipe, but if using a vinaigrette dressing, reheat the potatoes until just warm in a lidded pan or the microwave before adding the dressing – it always tastes better when applied to warm spuds.

nstant gratin

To be made only if the oven is being used for something else. Slice the potatoes and toss them in a gratin or baking dish with just enough cream to lubricate them well. Season with salt and pepper. Grate on some Cheddar, Gruyère or Emmenthal, and bake until the cheese is gold and bubbling, around 15 minutes.

dinner-party potatoes

It's Thursday night and you have people coming to dinner on Friday. You'll have plenty to do on Friday, so on Thursday cook a whole mess of new potatoes in the pressure cooker. Eat a couple for dinner, then dot the remainder around the roast – adding them 10–15 minutes before cooking is complete – or put them in a separate dish with butter, olive oil or duck fat. And some seasonings. No effort on Friday, a few pennies' worth of extra energy, and an impressive side dish.

crushed
hash browns

Crushed potatoes are usually served straight from the pot, but they're even better when refrigerated and treated to a little gentle frying. Put oil in a heavy frying pan to coat the bottom. Break the potatoes into a few rough pieces, drop them into the oil, then break them up a little more with a spatula. Add 1 slice of onion per potato (thin slice if the potatoes are tiny, thick if they're bigger) and season with salt and pepper. Fry over a moderate heat, with regular turning, for 6–8 minutes, until sizzling and golden.

favourite items of excess 2: rice

Properly cooked rice isn't mushy. It's soft, but the grains remain separate and retain a hint of bite.

As long as it hasn't been overcooked, it will reheat in a different form very admirably.

The easiest approaches are those that allow (or require) the rice to go all soft and squidgy, but you can also reheat it briefly so it softens without losing its bite.

Cooked rice should be cooled to room temperature and stored in the fridge overnight.

leftover soup

Put cooked rice in a large bowl with around 4 times its volume of stock, homemade or from a cube. Heat in the microwave until the liquid is very hot and the rice very soft. In the meantime, chop some cooked vegetables into fine dice. Add them to the soup just to heat through, around 1–2 minutes.

quicker congee

There is a 'proper' congee recipe in the chapter on pressure cookers (page 133). To make the same dish using leftovers, just put everything in the pot but use chunks of chicken or slivers of beef. Cook for 5 minutes, then release the pressure gradually.

oupy rice

This is a cross between rice and sauce. Gently cook some garlic and seasonings in a little butter, then put the rice in with enough stock or water (and a splash of wine) to cover by 2–3cm or so. Cook it until the rice is soft and the mixture very soupy. Serve with any plainly cooked fish, meat or poultry.

ried rice

Use 1 teaspoon plain vegetable or peanut oil per 100ml of cooked rice. Don't add anything wet until the dish is cooked. Stir-fry vegetables (if using) in the pan before cooking the rice, then remove them to a bowl. Fry the rice and when it is done, add the veg and a modest amount of sesame oil.

ice pudding

My mother used leftover rice in this way, and now I do too. Put the rice in a small saucepan (if it isn't there already) and break up any clumps with a fork. Add milk to cover, a suitable pinch of cinnamon powder, sugar to taste, and – if you wish – a small handful of raisins. Bring to the boil, clamp the lid on and simmer till the rice is perfectly soft (around 5–10 minutes). You may wish to add more milk for a looser texture, or a dollop of cream or Greek-style yogurt.

making the most of your oven

piggybacking in the oven

No, I'm not referring to a merry game played in the oven. Piggybacking means making one dish hitch a ride in the oven while the oven is on for another reason. The piggybacker can be another dish for tonight's meal or something you'll save for another day. Your oven eats energy the way Homer Simpson eats doughnuts: voraciously. The less you use it, the less energy it will consume. And if you have to use it, you can get the most out of it by taking a few simple measures.

flexible temperatures

Recipes give you an oven temperature to use when roasting or baking. In some cases, they are ignored only at your peril. Pastry and bread are the best known examples of foods that need a minimum temperature to rise and crisp and cook through quickly enough. But most other foods can be cooked at a lower or higher temperature than you read in your recipe, and you should remember this when you're piggybacking. If you're roasting a chicken at 200°C/400°F/ gas mark 6, you can cook anything where the recipe calls for temperatures up to 50°C lower or higher. You just need to pay closer attention to the cooking time for the other item(s).

think before you turn that dial

Does the dish you're planning on making really need to be cooked in the oven? Look at the chapter on Lidded Cooking (page 28) to see if there are alternatives. And if you're planning on cooking just one item in the oven, can you reconsider? Unless it's something huge that can only be roasted, like a turkey or a big rib of beef, there may be an alternative that doesn't use so much energy.

maximising oven use

If it's going to go on, get the most out of it by cooking more than one dish there. Dish number two can be something else for the same meal (vegetables, potatoes, dessert etc.) or it can be another meal for another day. Remember: the oven uses more energy, minute for minute, in preheating than in cooking. Adding another dish to the pre-heated oven will cause a brief spurt of energy use, then the thermostat will switch off the energy as it gets back to the required temperature.

planning oven meals

If the oven is going to be on for cooking a big main dish, such as a roast or casserole, it's easy to plan on cooking other dishes in the remaining space. Here are a few of the prime examples.

- Roast potatoes
- Baked potatoes
- Potato gratin
- Oven-cooked risotto or Spanish-style rice
- Roasted or braised vegetables
- Desserts, such as baked apples, crumbles, fruit tarts or pies, chocolate tart

a word about grills

Ovens aren't the only place in the kitchen where you can do some piggybacking.

If you're using the grill to cook some lamb cutlets, for instance, and you have spare room, you can use the room for another dish – a grilled pepper, courgettes, tomatoes etc. Never let any spare energy go to waste. Here is a sample menu.

A large, flat field mushroom drizzled with oil and vinegar and cooked under the grill as soon as you turn it on – around 5 minutes.
A medium courgette, halved and sprayed or brushed with oil and cooked under the grill as soon as you turn it on – around 5 minutes.
Your cutlets – 5–10 minutes.

I would put the vegetables on first, since they can wait for the lamb to get finished while the lamb can't wait a single second. This should add 2–3 minutes to the total grilling time, which is a small price to pay for cooking a full meal using a single pan or tin and a single energy source.

nixtures
nd sauces

Every home cook has a different list of items that see frequent use. I use homemade stock constantly. And softened vegetables resembling the French mirepoix, and Italian soffrito. But if you have your own list of always-in-use items, you should always make them in excess.

péchamel

chamel is one of the most useful sauces in European cookery, and one of best. The key point is to use equal quantities of butter and flour. chamel can be made to a thin 'pouring' consistency or thicker depending the eventual use. A thick version is better for long-term storage (less space eded in fridge or freezer), so that's what I've done here.

g butter
g plain flour
tre milk, whole or
emi-skimmed
ay leaf
hick slice of onion
and freshly ground
lack pepper

Melt the butter in a thick-bottomed saucepan and whisk in the flour. Cook gently, with constant whisking, until the flour and butter form a thick, creamy paste; this shouldn't take much more than a couple of minutes.

Now pour on around a quarter of the milk and whisk it in thoroughly until the lumps have disappeared. Add the rest of the milk and whisk constantly until the lumps go away. Put in the bay leaf and onion, season with salt and pepper and cook over a low heat until the mixture is thick enough to coat the back of a spoon, around 10 minutes. Stir it a few times, especially towards the end of cooking.

béchamel – the microwave method

The microwave, in my experience, doesn't do so well with large quantities of béchamel as a saucepan. Use half the quantity of all the ingredients and work as follows. This procedure is adapted from the *Good Housekeeping Microwave Handbook*.

Put the milk and flour in a large measuring jug and whisk thoroughly. Add all the remaining ingredients and cook at full power for 5–6 minutes, whisking after every minute. Strain and store as for the conventional method on page 161.

some béchamel variations

mornay sauce

Stir in a small handful of grated cheese per 500ml of sauce; mature Cheddar and Gruyère are top choices.

velouté sauce

Use chicken stock instead of milk. Note: in the classic French canon of saucery, velouté is usually considered a sauce in its own right.

mustard sauce

Stir in a small spoonful of smooth French or English mustard per 500ml of sauce.

herbed béchamel

Add 1 teaspoon dried mixed herbs, e.g. herbes de Provence.

butternut squash
with béchamel

Halve and deseed the squash and cook in the microwave for around 8–10 minutes, until perfectly soft. Spoon a good dollop of defrosted béchamel into the cavities of the squash for the last couple of minutes of cooking. Grated Parmesan or Gruyère, melted on top of the squash, and a sprinkling of chopped herbs or spring onions, will add extra bite. Each squash half will serve one or two people.

creamy vegetables

Except that they contain no cream – the luxurious richness comes from béchamel. Put the vegetables, anything you like, in a frying pan, with a good knob of butter. Heat it to melt the butter and season with salt and pepper. Add as much béchamel as you like, say around 2 tablespoons per 250g veg. Clamp the lid on and cook for 3–5 minutes, or until the vegetables are done the way you like them. Grate on some cheese, and if you're using the grill for something anyway, flash the cooked vegetables under it briefly to brown the top. And if you are using the oven anyway, the vegetables can be baked like a gratin.

new potatoes in white sauce

serves 4–6

around 500g new potatoes,
    washed and halved
1 medium onion, coarsely chopped
béchamel, to cover
salt and freshly ground
    black pepper
fresh herbs (optional)

The trick here is to cook the spuds in béchamel to cover them, so they are effectively simmered in the stuff, but then serve them with a slotted spoon so most of the sauce remains in the pot. It can then be used for the next recipe.

Put the potatoes and onion in a saucepan just large enough to hold them and add enough béchamel to cover. Season with salt and pepper, bring to the boil, then cover the pot and simmer gently until the potatoes are just cooked, around 20 minutes. Serve with a slotted spoon, and sprinkle each serving with finely chopped herbs, if you wish.

quick parsnip gratin

This is a deeply delicious and soothing side dish for grilled meat, especially lamb. And it can be made with potatoes as well as parsnips. Whichever you use, brown the top once the meat is finished – it just takes a minute or so.

Serves 4

2 large parsnips (around 650g),
    peeled, cored and cut in thin
    slices or batons
around 300ml béchamel
salt and freshly ground
    black pepper
a little grated nutmeg
a large handful of grated Cheddar,
    Gruyère or another hard cheese

Put the parsnips in a large, non-stick frying pan with the béchamel and some salt and pepper. Grate the nutmeg on evenly, then clamp the lid on and bring to a boil over a medium heat. Cook until the parsnips are perfectly soft (around 10 minutes). Leave, covered, for up to 10 minutes.

Put all the cheese on in an even layer and put the pan under the grill. Cook until the cheese is brown and crusty, around 1–2 minutes. Serve immediately.

sauce soubise

Béchamel is also the basis for dozens of variant sauces. For my money, the pick of the litter is sauce soubise, which goes well with an alarming number of dishes: meat (especially lamb), poultry, fish, baked potatoes, lidded or microwaved vegetables. The quantities here will sauce four or five separate dishes, and naturally you can increase the quantities if you want an even bigger supply for the freezer. Both béchamel and sauce soubise can be frozen in ice-cube trays if you sometimes want to use just a little bit of them. When the cubes are frozen, transfer them to plastic tubs and seal tightly.

2 large Spanish onions
  (around 400g each)
60g butter
900ml milk
1 bay leaf
2 tablespoons plain flour
a good pinch of cayenne
a good pinch of freshly
  grated nutmeg
½ teaspoon dried thyme
salt and freshly ground
  black pepper

Chop or slice the onions and melt the butter over a low heat in a heavy-bottomed saucepan. Cover the pot and cook the onions, stirring regularly, until good and soft. Don't think you can rush this! It takes at least 30 minutes. Just remember that they should not brown.

While they are cooking, bring the milk and bay leaf to a simmer in a small saucepan. Some writers say that scalded milk guarantees a lump-less sauce, but I've never noticed a difference.

When the onions are soft, add the flour, seasonings and some salt and pepper. Mix well and cook, stirring constantly with a wooden spoon, until the flour is completely absorbed. Now pour in the hot milk, stir vigorously, and simmer until the sauce is thick enough to coat the back of the spoon, around 20–30 minutes. Stir every few minutes, scraping the pan to prevent sticking. Purée in a blender and pass through a fine sieve if you want a perfectly smooth sauce. If you want the onions' texture in the sauce, leave it as it is.

Cooked sauce can be held for a while if covered, or filmed with a little milk or butter, to prevent the formation of a skin. Reheat as necessary, and freeze in containers that will hold around 200–250ml of sauce.

offrito

offrito is the Italian mixture of sweated onions, garlic and celery that forms
e basis for dozens of sauces, stews and soups. Sometimes it also includes
rrots. It keeps well in the fridge for a week, and almost indefinitely in the
ezer. That's why the recipe here is for an absolutely massive quantity.

arge onions,
inely chopped
arge knob of butter
nd a generous slug (around
75ml) of extra virgin olive oil
jarlic cloves, finely chopped
5 sticks of celery, trimmed
nd finely chopped
arge or 6 small carrots,
inely chopped
and freshly ground
black pepper

Put the onions in a large, heavy saucepan or (better) a large,
heavy frying pan; the frying pan will cook the soffrito faster.
Put in the butter and oil and turn the heat on. Stirring
everything together, let the butter melt and the oil get hot
enough to sizzle the onions, then turn the heat down low
and cook until the onions start to become very fragrant.

Add the garlic and cook for a few more minutes, until it
too becomes very fragrant. Now add all the remaining
ingredients, season with salt and pepper and cook over the
same very low heat, with frequent stirring and tossing, until
the mixture is soft but retaining a hint of bite. This can take
anything from 20–30 minutes for a large quantity.

To freeze soffrito, pack it into small containers filling nearly
to the top; you want to prevent air contact, but you also
need to leave a little room for expansion. It keeps well for
several months.

how to use it: a few suggestions

As a base for any tomato sauce
As an addition to pulses or rice
Mix into meatloaf, pâté or hamburgers
As a base for vegetable soups

167

a simple tomato sauce

This freezes well, almost indefinitely.

100ml extra virgin olive oil
200ml soffrito (see page 167)
2 teaspoon mixed dried herbs,
  such as herbes de Provence
2 bay leaves
a pinch of chilli powder (optional)
2 tablespoons tomato purée
6 x 400g tins chopped tomatoes
  or 2½ kg fresh, ripe tomatoes

Put all the ingredients except the tomatoes in a large bowl (for the microwave) or in a large saucepan if you prefer to cook it on the hob. Heat for a couple of minutes at high power in the microwave, stirring a few times, or stir over a low heat in a saucepan. Now stir in the tomatoes and cook at medium power in the microwave for 12–15 minutes, stirring every couple of minutes, until the sauce has reduced to a thick sludge. In the saucepan it will take anything from 30–45 minutes.

seasonal gluts, suburban-style

When people lived on farms and grew their own vegetables, they became experts at taking advantage of seasonal gluts: those moments in the year, principally summer and autumn, when crops were ready for harvest and had to be used or left to go rotten. They learned how to pickle, preserve, and make chutneys, jams, sauces and ketchups. The principle of seasonal glut still exists, and it can be exploited even if you've never walked in a farmyard, let alone worked in one. Here are a few tips.

When fresh herbs are very cheap at the summer's end, buy in bulk and preserve, after coarsely chopping them, in ice cubes or cubes of frozen vegetable oil.

Unsightly, unevenly sized late-summer tomatoes can sometimes be found selling for next to nothing. They make great tomato sauce (see above) and can be frozen if you're not up to putting them in sterilised jars.

Single-vegetable purées are a good thing to freeze in smallish containers for use in small servings of sauce or soup. Puréed tomatoes are great for this, though courgettes, peppers and squash can be treated in the same way. Defrost a cupful, heat it with some garlic or spring onions, add a dollop of yogurt or crème fraîche – instant soup.

stock

Stock is something you can make as well at home as they make it in any professional kitchen. Since it takes no more energy or washing-up to produce 5 litres than to produce 1 litre, large-scale stock-making is the only type a green cook should contemplate. My approach is very simple, though it does require large quantities of the meat and bones. If you can only get them a little bit at a time, freeze them until you have enough.

around 2.5kg meaty scraps
3–4 garlic cloves
1 medium onion, topped
  and tailed
2 bay leaves
1 stick of celery (or, better still,
  the washed tops of several
  sticks with the leaves intact)
2 bay leaves
a few black peppercorns
a few good pinches of
  dried mixed herbs –
  herbes de Provence

Put the scraps in a very large pot and cover with cold water by around 5cm. Bring to a good steady simmer – do not let it boil hard – and watch for a few minutes until the whitish-grey scum starts to rise. Turn the heat down to low at this point. Skim off the scum using a slotted spoon and keep watching for more of it. When it has stopped appearing on the top, put in all the remaining ingredients and let the stock simmer gently for 2 hours or so. You can tell when the stock is ready by lifting out a scrap; if the meat is falling off the bone and has little or no taste in it, the stock is ready. Turn off the heat.

Ladle the stock into a clean saucepan through a fine-mesh strainer, preferably one in which you have placed a piece of muslin, folded to make 4 layers, or a clean and odour-free tea-towel. Place over a low heat and simmer gently to reduce it – this makes it more compact for the freezer – by around one quarter to one half. While it's reducing, degrease it using a ladle to skim off the fat from the top. When it's reduced, pour it into small containers and freeze as soon as possible. Some people like freezing stock in ice cube trays, but I personally never use as little as a cube, so I prefer small plastic tubs.

soup base

his is one of the most useful things you can have in your freezer. You can
eeze it in serving-size parcels to make the basis for a quick lunch, with the
up completed by the addition of chicken stock. You can vary the
roportions and ingredients almost endlessly.

medium leeks
medium onions
medium carrots
large (i.e. baking size) potatoes
head of celery
large turnip
0g tin good-quality plum
tomatoes
rbs and spices, see below
ck, see below

note on herbs and spices: This
up base can be flavoured with
atever you like, but you should
r on the side of mild seasoning so
u increase the versatility of the
xture for subsequent uses.

ck: Water will do. Vegetable
ck will be better. Chicken stock,
en from stock cubes, will be better
l. If you can flavour the liquid with
me meat bones or a bit of bacon,
the better.

Cut all the vegetables into bite-sized pieces. Put them into
a pot large enough to hold everything and stir.

You now need to add liquid, and this should be the most
flavourful liquid you can manage (see left). The important
thing is to put in just enough liquid barely to cover the
vegetables. They will be stewing, not boiling. You can
now put the pot over a low heat on the hob. You can also
cook it in the oven, as long as you are using the oven
for something else. At 150°C/300°F/gas mark 4, this
quantity of vegetables took me just under 1 hour to cook
to melting softness. In your oven, it may take 15 minutes
more or less than that – but it will happen easily, and with
little extra expenditure of energy.

There's another way to cook this: in the pressure cooker.
It will take around 5 minutes with slow release (see page
101), and the results are perfect.

Instant vegetable curry
Fry onions, garlic and curry powder in a frying pan or
saucepan and add as much soup base as you need.
Cook just long enough to heat through.

A base for roast or grilled chicken
Heat the base in the microwave and put it on heated
serving plates using a slotted spoon to drain off some of
the liquid. Plonk the chicken on top and sprinkle with
chopped fresh herbs. The base acts as something like a
cross between a side dish and a sauce.

Vegetable patties
Drain the base of excess liquid and mix with dried
breadcrumbs and a beaten egg (or two). Form into thick
patties and fry in vegetable oil until crisp on the outside.

whole dishes

When you're cooking whole dishes for later reuse, you have to be a little bit careful. Some foods simply don't take well to freezing once they are cooked: the texture suffers too much to make them truly appetising. Chicken and fish are prime examples; pasta is another. But that still leaves you with ample choice, of which my two favourites are pulses and braised meat dishes.

Pulses freeze perfectly. Their texture may end up being on the soft and mushy side, but that's not really a problem for most dishes where they're used, with the obvious exception of salads. Once they've been frozen, you wouldn't really want to use them for that anyway.

simple lentils

1kg lentils, preferably Puy
100ml extra virgin olive oil
200ml soffrito (see page 167)
2 teaspoon mixed dried herbs, such as herbes de Provence
2 bay leaves
a pinch of chilli powder (optional)
2 tablespoons tomato purée
2 x 400g tins chopped tomatoes

Wash the lentils, saving the water for your house plants or garden. Cook the soffrito briefly, just to heat it through. Then add all the remaining ingredients. Bring to the boil and simmer gently, covered, until the lentils are done, 25–30 minutes. Check the pot from time to time and top up with stock, or water, if necessary.

Alternative method: the pressure cooker. Cook the lentils for 7 minutes once full pressure has been reached, and release the steam immediately if you want them to be very al dente.

entils with fennel
nd red peppers

can make Simple Lentils even better when you're eating them a second
hird time. Here is a sample suggestion, but you should create your own
iants according to what you happen to have on hand.

 fennel
pepper
onion
 coriander
ek yogurt or crème fraîche

Simply dice the vegetables, chop the coriander and mix
with the lentils. Then add the yogurt or crème fraîche and
mix well.

three days of beans

You should always cook too many beans, whether for freezing or shorter storage in the fridge. They're reheatable just as they come out of storage, but they're even better when you fool around and transform them into something completely different. Here is a three-day bean extravaganza that I particularly like. The dishes are so different that no one will object to eating them three days in a row – well, maybe they won't object. If they do, just freeze the beans and serve the second and third days after an acceptable interval.

day one

The Braised Beans recipe on page 119, but doubled in quantity and cooked in the oven at 150°C/300°F/gas mark 3 for around 2 hours.

Tuscan-style bean soup

With crusty bread this will serve 4 as a main course, 6–8 as a starter.

Tablespoons extra virgin
olive oil
garlic cloves, finely chopped
sun-dried tomatoes,
finely chopped
sticks of celery, finely chopped
Savoy cabbage leaves,
shredded
tablespoon red wine vinegar
tablespoon tomato purée
litre chicken or vegetable stock
around 1kg cooked cannellini beans
few paper-thin slices of red
onion (optional)
small handful of fresh parsley,
roughly chopped

Put the oil in a large saucepan or casserole, add the garlic, sun-dried tomatoes, celery and cabbage and gently cook for a few minutes. Add the vinegar, purée and stock, and simmer for 30 minutes or cook in the pressure cooker for 3 minutes with immediate venting.

Put a quarter of the beans into your blender with a spoonful of stock from the vegetables. Purée roughly, and add to the pot along with the remaining beans. Simmer for another 30–45 minutes, or cook in the pressure cooker for 5 minutes, until the flavours are blended and the vegetables perfectly soft. Serve with the onion slices, if using, and parsley on top.

spicy bean patties

Vaguely inspired by the Sabzi Kabab recipe in Julie Sahni's *Classic Indian Vegetarian Cooking*. Any resemblance to 'veggie burgers' is purely coincidental. Serves 4 as a main course with an assortment of vegetables, 8 as a side dish, and cucumber raita makes a good accompaniment.

vegetable oil
½ teaspoon ground cumin
1 teaspoon ground coriander
½ teaspoon cayenne
150g onions, finely chopped
1 fresh green chilli,
  finely chopped
a large (1.5cm or so) cube
  of fresh ginger, peeled
  and finely chopped
750g cooked cannellini beans
juice of ½ lemon
200g fresh white breadcrumbs
  (around 6 thick slices from
  a large loaf)
a large handful of fresh coriander,
  coarsely chopped

Heat around 1 tablespoon vegetable oil in a large frying pan and fry the spices for a minute or so, until they colour lightly, then turn the heat down and add the onions, chilli and ginger. Cook for 10 minutes, stirring every minute or so. Mix well with the beans, lemon juice, breadcrumbs and coriander, then form into 8 patties around 2cm thick. Refrigerate until needed.

To cook, heat enough oil in the pan to form a generous coating. Fry the patties in batches until crisp, 5–6 minutes per side; care will be needed in turning, especially if the mixture was very wet. The cooked patties can be kept hot in the oven until all of them are ready – but only if you're using the oven for something else anyway.

the multiple mindset

Before you're used to it, cooking for multiple meals can seem foreign and confusing. You are asking your brain to compartmentalise itself, so it can deal with the immediate task – dinner, soon – simultaneously with the extra task of cooking something for another day. I know from experience that this multi-tasking is not easy: I've been doing it for years and I still struggle sometimes to keep those multiple meals in logical order. But while it takes some time and effort to get used to thinking in this way, it gets easier once you've started. You just need to think about two different things: the type of extra food you want to cook, and the way you want to cook it. It isn't a mind-bending challenge, honest.

preparation in bulk

It isn't just cooking that can be done for multiple meals. Bulk preparation of the foods you often eat will save on time and washing up. I don't know what you eat frequently at home, so I will give an example from my own kitchen.

We eat a lot of chicken where I live: whole chicken, legs, wings, stir-fries and braises and sautés and kebabs. If I prepared the chicken every time I cooked it, I would have to wash a knife and chopping board every single time. Instead of doing that, I do at least a double dose of preparation whenever I'm cooking chicken. If I'm boning one for dinner, I bone another for freezing, which also gives me extra bones for making stock in bulk. Chicken in chunks is an even better bet, as you can freeze lots of them in bags or boxes for later use.

Freezing tip: freeze the pieces, making sure they don't touch each other, on a baking tray or non-stick baking sheet (see page 26). When they're frozen, transfer to boxes or bags. You will then be able to pull out just what you need, whether it's one piece or a dozen.

dual cooking, frying pan to oven

Chefs often tell you that simple meat dishes such as steaks, chops and poultry pieces should be seared in a frying pan (they may call it 'sealed', but this is wrong) and then transferred to the oven to complete the cooking. Professional kitchens do this frequently because (a) their ovens are always on, (b) they can monitor the cooking more easily that way, and (c) it is a very good way to cook. Nonetheless, it's annoying when they say this without remembering that domestic kitchens don't have an always-on oven. If you're turning on the oven just to complete the cooking of a few pork chops, you are not using your oven wisely.

If you are going to be using the oven anyway, however, two-stage cooking is a really excellent method. It gives useful latitude on cooking times, as the oven cooks the items more slowly than a frying pan, and it enables you to cook dishes for a crowd that would ordinarily be impractical. If you want to find out what I mean by impractical, just try frying or grilling 18 lamb cutlets to serve 6 people.

When using two-stage cooking in the Green Kitchen, you should get the oven going to cook whatever side dish(es) will take the longest time: baked potatoes, a gratin, roasted root vegetables etc. When they're nearly done, sear the meat in your frying pan two or three pieces at a time and transfer them to a roasting dish with a metal grill in place. When they're all done, put the dish in the oven to complete cooking for anything from 5 minutes or so (in a hot oven, over 200°C/400°F/gas mark 6) to 20 minutes or so (at around 130°C/250°F/gas mark ½).

meat

Tough cuts of meat, slowly cooked in the oven (or fast in the pressure cooker), are ideal for freezing because they come with a lot of stewing or braising liquid. When you freeze them, you just have to make sure they're covered by wet stuff. The air of the freezer can dry them out on the surface (freezer burn) if they're not covered. Freezer burn is safe to eat but doesn't improve the appearance or texture. The meat dishes in the pressure cooker chapter are suitable for this treatment. Here are two others. Make too much, freeze the remainder with a covering of liquid, and use in other dishes.

casserole of belly pork

8 strips of belly pork (about 1.5kg in total)
60ml peanut oil
2 garlic cloves, finely chopped
1 bay leaf
1 small chilli
1kg white cabbage, sliced into bite-sized pieces
2 tablespoons each of Worcestershire sauce, red wine vinegar and soy sauce
500ml chicken stock
2 x 400g tins plum tomatoes, drained and coarsely chopped
1 tablespoon tomato purée
a large pinch of thyme
salt and freshly ground black pepper

Preheat the oven to 175°C/325°F/gas mark 3.

Cut the pork into 10cm pieces. Heat the oil in a heavy casserole and gently fry the garlic, bay leaf and chilli for a minute or so. Add the cabbage to the casserole with the pork and the remaining ingredients. Season with salt and pepper, stir well, and bring to the boil. Cover and cook in the oven for 2 hours or so, stirring occasionally. Skim well and serve immediately with boiled rice.

This make 8 portions – eat what you need and freeze the rest.

shin of beef
with chinese-style sauce

shin is a deeply flavourful and nearly fat-less cut, tough as boot-leather but made succulent through long cooking. Here is a favourite recipe of mine, with leftover variations. Save the water for covering the beef when you freeze it.

serves 4–6, with plenty of leftovers

shin of beef, about 1.8kg, boned
large onion
large carrots
garlic cloves

for the sauce
large or 2 small green chillies, deseeded and finely chopped
garlic cloves, finely chopped
shallots or spring onions, finely chopped
good chunk of fresh ginger, peeled and finely chopped
0ml soy sauce
tablespoons red wine vinegar
tablespoons dry sherry
tablespoon sesame oil
tablespoon sugar
small handful of fresh coriander

In a stockpot, cover the shin with water by 5cm. Bring to the boil, skim, and add the vegetables. Simmer, partly covered, until the meat is tender when pierced; this will take around 3 hours and you'll need to top up the water as necessary to keep the meat covered. Leave the meat in the water until you're ready to eat.

To make the sauce, combine all the ingredients except the coriander, and let them mingle for 1 hour. At the last minute, chop and add the coriander.

Slice the meat thinly and lay it out on a serving platter. Moisten it with a ladle or so of the broth, and pass the sauce separately. Serve with boiled rice.

The leftovers should be covered completely with cooking liquid so they don't get exposed to air and suffer freezer burn as a result. Reheat gently and serve with a dipping sauce, or try the ideas below.

leftovers

pasta sauce
chop the meat finely and stir it into a tomato sauce a minute before serving.

beef, cucumber and radish salad
Slice the meat thinly. Cut thin slices of cucumber and radish and toss with spring onions and a vinaigrette made with 2 parts vegetable oil, 1 part sesame oil, and 1 part red wine vinegar. Put the beef around the vegetables or on top of them.

vegetable soup
Make any soup, from fresh or leftover vegetables, and chop the meat in small pieces. Add to the soup a minute or two before serving, just long enough to heat through.

a whole meal in the oven

It drives me slightly crazy when I see a recipe plan for a full meal that calls for cooking just one dish – sometimes even part of a dish – in the oven. Remember: the oven is a relatively inefficient place for cooking because it needs to use energy to heat up a large volume of air before the food can start cooking. If you're using the oven, use it for more than one dish.

Here is a quartet of recipes, a full meal for four people, with everything cooked in the oven. It's presented here not as a meal that you urgently need to make (though the dishes are all very good) but as an example of the kind of cooking you can do once you've started thinking multiply. For all the dishes, the oven temperature is 200°C/400°F/ gas mark 6.

menu

Starter
Roasted peppers with anchovies and capers

Main course
Roasted chicken pieces with lemon and cumin, served with Fennel and new potatoes with rosemary and garlic

Dessert
Peach cobbler, southern style

The cooking plan
- Get the peppers roasting
- Prepare the fennel and potatoes and add to the oven
- Prepare the chicken and add to the oven when the peppers are done
- Prepare the cobbler and cook it while you're eating

oasted peppers with
nchovies and capers

red peppers
anchovy fillets, drained and
roughly chopped
teaspoons capers, drained
and roughly chopped
shly ground black pepper
ound 50ml extra virgin olive oil
small handful of parsley,
finely chopped

Halve the peppers, remove the seeds and the white pith, and put them in a roasting tin. Mix the anchovies and capers with a good grinding of black pepper and divide them equally between the 8 pepper halves. Drizzle the oil over the peppers, using more if you want a really luxurious effect.

Put the peppers in the oven and roast until soft and slightly blackened around the edges – around 30 minutes. While they are cooking, prepare the other vegetables.

fennel and new potatoes with rosemary and garlic

500g small new potatoes
a large sprig of fresh rosemary
4 small or medium fennel bulbs,
  trimmed and halved
around 2 tablespoons extra
  virgin olive oil
salt and freshly ground
  black pepper
1–2 garlic cloves, peeled and
  finely chopped

Put the potatoes in a large roasting tin with the sprig of rosemary buried under them.

Put the fennel on top and drizzle oil over everything. Add a splash of water, season with salt and pepper and put the tin in the oven. Roast with occasional basting, aiming to keep the fennel from drying out or getting excessively blackened. The spuds and fennel should both take around 30 minutes, but you may want to take the fennel out earlier – that's the reason for putting it on top.

When the potatoes are just about done, scatter the garlic on top, baste again, and roast for another few minutes – just long enough to complete the cooking and heat the garlic to full fragrance.

roasted chicken pieces with lemon and cumin

4 chicken quarters, breasts
  or (preferably) legs
2 lemons, thinly sliced and
  pips removed
1 teaspoon whole cumin seeds
50ml dry white wine
salt and freshly ground
  black pepper

Trim any excess fat from the chicken. Remove the peppers from their roasting tin and put them on the serving plates. Now give the tin a quick rinse and put the lemon slices in the bottom (you don't need to dry it). Scatter the cumin seeds evenly over the lemon. Put the chicken pieces in, pour in the wine with an equal quantity of water, and season with salt and pepper. Roast for around 30 minutes, basting occasionally and checking the liquid levels; add more water or wine if the pan is drying out. This can be eaten straight from the oven or at something between oven-hot and lukewarm.

each cobbler, southern style

the topping
g plain flour
teaspoons baking powder
blespoons sugar
aspoon salt
unsalted butter
l single cream
rge egg

the fruit
nerous knob of unsalted butter
rge, ripe peaches, stoned,
ced, and tossed with the
ice of ½ lemon
sugar
aspoon cinnamon powder

To make the topping, sift the dry ingredients into a mixing bowl, then cut in the butter until the mixture resembles coarse breadcrumbs. Beat in the cream and egg until just smooth.

For the fruit, smear a baking dish around 20cm square with the butter. Toss the peaches with the sugar and cinnamon and spread out evenly in the dish. Drop the topping onto the fruit in large spoonfuls, leaving spaces so the peaches are partly visible. Bake in the upper third of the oven until the topping is golden-brown, around 20–25 minutes. Serve hot with cream, whipped cream or vanilla ice cream.

7.greener cleaning

A kitchen has to be clean, needless to say. This is especially true of any surface used in food preparation, or which might come into contact with uncooked foods. Does that mean it has to be treated like a surgical theatre and disinfected with legions of chemicals? No. There are greener ways of doing it, which will keep you from releasing chemicals into the environment and will also, in the long run, save you a great deal of money.

serving the green meal

In years gone by, when I cooked a dinner for family or friends, I removed the food from a cooking vessel to a serving vessel. Without thinking about it, I was adding two, four, six or eight extra dishes to the washing-up list for the end of the evening.

Why did I do it? Pride, I suppose. How more un-cool can you be than to serve mashed potatoes in a stainless steel saucepan? Well, un-cool it may be. But if you reckon that un-cool means ultra-green, is there a serious choice to be made? By not getting out a serving bowl for those spuds, you are eliminating one item from your washing-up agenda. In a dinner party for 6 people, that might mean dozens of litres of water. Plus the energy to heat the water. Plus the washing-up liquid.

Slimmed-down service also makes serving easier, since pots with a handle are easier to pass than those that don't have one. You just need a trivet under them if they're still hot.

It isn't just pots and pans that work well on the dinner table: dishes cooked in the microwave are natural candidates for slimmed-down service, as cooking dish and serving dish are one and the same. The same applies to roasting tins full of baked root vegetables or roasted peppers.

This is an opportunity to re-examine the whole distinction between cookware and tableware. The best modern cookware is beautiful stuff. Go on, show it off to your guests.

efficient washing-up

The wrong way to wash dishes: hold the brush under a gushing tap while you scrub plates, glasses and cutlery. You're washing away the cleaning liquid and will need to use much more of it.

What's the right way to wash dishes? This question has been studied by scientists at the University of Bonn, and they have described a method that they call 'super-economic' hand-washing. The main points:

• Clear off large scraps

• Wash dishes soon after eating

• Don't pre-rinse under running water

• Use two water-filled sinks – hot and soapy to wash, cold to rinse

That may work for you, as long as you have a double sink. If you use a bowl or sink of hot water for the initial wash, plan carefully the order in which you wash things.

Put in lightly soiled items first – drinking glasses for example. Then splash water onto the top of plates and wash them without getting the bottoms dirty. The final items should be heavily soiled stuff, especially frying pans with lots of burnt-on bits and cooking oil or fat. See also the notes on stacking your plates on page 190.

eusing pots and pans

When you use a pot or pan, you wash it. Right? Not necessarily. If it is caked with carbonised animal protein, yes. Or if it's coated with oil, fat or cooking residues which would render unpalatable the next dish cooked in it. In many other instances, washing is wasteful.

If you're like me, you use certain cooking vessels regularly for certain purposes. My principal example is a stainless steel pot used almost exclusively for cooking pasta. That pot gets an outing at least once a week, and washing it after each use would waste time, water and energy. When the cooked pasta is dumped out, all that remains is a whitish residue combining dissolved starch with mineral precipitates from the water. I don't call that truly dirty, especially since the next thing in there will be more water and more penne. Now the pot rarely meets soap and hot water. The main treatment: a quick swishing-out (scrubbing optional) while it's still hot.

I treat my steamer in a similar manner. The only grime it acquires is dripping water from the vegetables (which can be used a couple of times, by the way). When the water starts looking pond-like, I just scour the pot with a steel pad – cold-water rinse, no washing-up liquid.

By not washing these two vessels every time I use them, I save around 200 litres of water per annum. Plus washing-up liquid and the energy to heat the water. That may not sound like much, but look at it this way. The average UK household uses around 140 litres per person of water a day. Over the course of a year, with one simple, slothful step, I am effectively shaving $1\frac{1}{3}$ days of water use off my annual total.

stacking

Stacking dirty dishes is the worst thing you can do in the Green Kitchen. It's fine if the dishes will eventually go into the dishwasher, but if you're stacking things that have to be hand washed, you may be dirtying what was not dirty before.

Serving bowls and cookware are prime examples. If you put them in the sink, then fill the sink with water, you are coating the clean bottoms and sides with greasy water. You'll need twice as much hot water and soap to clean them. The solution? If you're not washing up straight after a dinner party finishes, leave large bowls, pots and pans on the hob or on the table, with their outer surfaces away from water or cooking grime. Plates are trickier if your kitchen space is limited, so it's best to stack them in pairs. Just wipe them well first with a used paper towel or a tea-towel that's ready to go into the washing machine. The next day, they'll be easy to wash by hand.

The most important point in the green washing regime is not to make anything dirtier when storing it in readiness for washing. Putting a water glass in a bowl of water with a greasy frying pan is sheer folly.

soaking

Some cooking pots end up with a burnt-on layer of crud thick and tough enough to stop a bullet. In the old days, I would have filled the pot with hot water and a large sploosh of washing-up liquid, and left it to soak. Now I know better. That long soak is an unnecessary waste of water (as much as 10–20 litres), energy and soap.

The green alternative? Replace the soak with a serious scouring pad, a couple of cups-worth of cold water, and a minute or two of good exercise for the upper arm. Pour water into pot. Don plastic kitchen glove and dip scouring pad into water. Rub pot fiercely wherever crud adheres. Rinse pad out occasionally. Soon the crud will all be in the water. Tip out water. Wash and rinse normally.

The best scouring pad is the cheap, brutish type resembling razor wire, sold in hardware stores, Asian food shops and catering supply shops. Hand-friendlier pads of soft metal or plastic are good enough, but they prolong your work because they are not nearly so sharp. If it must be plastic, Heavy Duty Scotch-Brite™ Scouring Pads (polyester coated with aluminium oxide) are top choice.

Remember also that powerful scourers can scratch enamel linings in addition to releasing noxious chemicals into the water supply. Proceed cautiously with enamel.

For non-stick pans, use a polyester or nylon scouring pad such as ordinary Scotch-Brite™.

Finally: some people just can't get over the soaking habit. If you are one of them, wash other dishes while holding them over the soak-worthy pot, so the washing water fills it. In the Green Kitchen, water is never, ideally, used just once.

ashing-up brushes

Every Green Kitchen needs two washing-up brushes. Here's the rationale.

Some dishes need to be washed in two stages, the first being removal of heavy grime. Coagulated scrambled eggs, clingy sauces, meaty or tomato-ey fragments from pasta – that kind of thing. The second stage removes filmy grime: a clear coating, usually oily, with very fine traces of particulate matter.

Stage one is really a scrub rather than a clean, using no washing-up liquid and barely any water. This is what the old brush is for. If you use your newer brush, the particles will cling to the bristles and you will have to remove them before you do the real washing.

When the heavy matter is removed, out come new brush, washing-up liquid, hot water. Bristles remain clear, and less soap and water are needed because you're not constantly having to rinse off accumulated crud.

NB: you can use a scrubbing pad for the first cleaning, but this means putting on a rubber glove or getting your hands filthy. Filthy hands = more soap and water. NB also: using two brushes is good food-safety practice. Large particles don't even touch the newer one, let alone cling to its bristles for days on end.

Eventually, the newer brush will give up the ghost. It then becomes the backup brush and you have to buy a new brush for front-line duty.

cleaning agents

Millions practise what I call Scorched Earth Cleaning (SEC). In the SEC world-view, which manufacturers do their utmost to promote, you need to use apocalyptically powerful cleansing agents on every kitchen work surface or your family will fall prey to all manner of malevolent bacteria. We put around 500 million litres of chemical waste down our drains every year. This is simply unnecessary. A number of well-meaning companies have launched cleaning products designed as alternatives to SEC. Their green credentials usually rest on the use of plant-based, biodegradable ingredients, and/or on minimal and recyclable packaging. Some are sold in concentrated form, which means that less fossil fuel is needed in transport. They can be sprays, wipes and concentrated cleaners.

The rationale behind buying concentrates is particularly sound. Did you ever think about how much fossil fuel is used to ship hundreds of thousands of plastic bottles filled with a liquid comprising over 98 per cent water? In one green concentrate product I've used, the empty bottle weighs 77g; filled, it weighs 772g.

That's a lot less water-weight being shipped around the country. And these refillable bottles are all-plastic and therefore recyclable whereas most conventional spray bottles incorporate a metal spring.

But I still can't recommend any commercial cleaner beyond the washing-up liquid you already use. Some work fairly well, but no better than washing-up liquid. While I would choose them happily over conventional Scorched Earth Cleaners, they're not as good as microfibre cloths.

Two other cleaning agents deserve a mention here: clear vinegar and bicarbonate of soda, used separately or together. Both are fully biodegradable and cheap.

The acid in vinegar has antibacterial properties, so it's a good disinfectant – just as effective in some studies as industrially produced cleaning agents. Try to buy it in a large jug (less cost and less packaging) but apply it from spray bottle of the kind you use for spraying plants with water. The smell of the vinegar doesn't linger long, just in case you're worrying that your house will smell like salad dressing.

Bicarbonate of soda is an alkaline crystal better known for its uses in baking. It's coarse and abrasive and makes a good scouring powder for stainless steel sinks, splashbacks and draining boards. Don't buy the small tubs sold in the supermarket; hardware stores and some online suppliers sell larger boxes which work out much cheaper.

Better than vinegar or bicarbonate is the two of them working together. You can combine them either by sprinkling bicarbonate on a surface and then spraying with vinegar, or by mixing them in a small bowl or plastic tub. When mixed, they froth up excitedly. And the froth works wonders on limescale, heavy grease, even the carbonised residues on oven walls or barbecue grids. It's also a chemical-free drain clearer: pour a cup of bicarbonate down the drain, followed by 200ml or so of vinegar. Listen to the bubbling, then go away for 30 minutes. Come back and flush with hot water from the tap.

clean sink

The kitchen sink gets at least its share of SEC – cream cleansers and the like. Is this necessary? Not according to Ian Connerton, Northern Foods Professor of Food Safety in the Biosciences Department of the University of Nottingham. Cleaning the sink every day, though 'not imperative', is 'good practice'. A dirty sink is not necessarily hazardous, but splashes from the tap can carry out pathogenic bacteria 'as an aerosol.' This is one good reason not to wash poultry; another good reason is that you don't need to. Professor Connerton's alternative? 'Soap and hot water.' There's no need for the more expensive and environmentally damaging SEC measures. And never use corrosive cleaners on a stainless steel sink, he adds: they can etch the steel and provide a safe haven for bacteria.

dishwasher use

In a customer review of a salad spinner, spotted on Amazon, I read the following statement in praise of a particular spinner: 'It's dishwasher-proof. I refuse to buy any kitchen aid that's not.' What idiocy. If ever there was a kitchen appliance that does not need to go into a dishwasher, it's the salad spinner. First of all, salad spinners barely get dirty. They usually don't need washing with soap at all. Second, the size and shape of these essential utensils makes them brilliantly unsuited to the dishwasher.

The same applies, needless to say, with any large pot, frying pan, bowl or oven dish. If it's taking up too much space, wash it by hand.

You will be justifying the purchase of a dishwasher if you follow the two basic principles of dishwasher use.

• Don't run the dishwasher till it's full. If you have a full-size dishwasher, you need sufficient plates and cutlery to use while you're waiting to fill it. If you don't have enough tableware, you will be digging around in the dishwasher to find the dishes you need – and then washing them by hand. Or worse still, you will be tempted to run the machine when it's less than full, which negates the water-savings of modern efficient dishwashers (see page 9).

• Fill the machine efficiently. If you have a full-size model machine, you may be tempted to pack it with things like colanders and casseroles (or salad spinners!) just so you can run it at a reasonable interval to get plates and spoons clean. A large saucepan can occupy the space used by 6 or 8 plates. Washing those big things in the dishwasher is a major waste of water and energy, again negating the water-savings from the machine.

nicro-miracles

Microfibre cloth is a remarkable Swedish product made of microscopically fine filaments cut with tiny wedges that trap whatever they touch. According to a report on the website of Microfibre Cleaning Solutions, they also disinfect using no cleaning agents. All you need to use with them is water. And it doesn't even have to be hot water. How's that for green?

A number of products call themselves Microfibre. According to Nicky Shaw of Microfibre Cleaning Solutions, not all of them have those filth-trapping wedges. My experience bears this out: some microfibre cloths I've used worked less well, and died at a younger age. But the safest way to be sure of buying good quality is to spend more – a cheap microfibre cloth is likely to clean less efficiently and die sooner.

The best microfibre cloths (the best known brand is E-Cloth) leave even the yuckiest steel dry, shiny, and grease-free. They use no chemicals and require no spray bottles (though the E-Cloth company sells one, for people who need to squeeze). The more I use this stuff, the more convinced I am that the Clean 'n' Green Kitchen needs nothing more than microfibre cloths, water and ordinary washing-up liquid for most cleaning jobs.

Microfibre cloths are machine-washable up to 200 or 300 times before they start losing their powers. If you use them as your kitchen-cleaner of choice, you will get them dirty often. Solution: buy at least two cloths, if not half a dozen (they're good for cleaning every part of your house). If you have a lot of them, you will always have at least one clean one in the kitchen. And being small and thin, they take up no extra room in the washing machine so you're not using extra resources to clean them. A cloth or two can join a full load of laundry without over-burdening the machine. Use it regularly and you'll soon realise that most plastic bottles, apart from the one containing washing-up liquid in, are *de trop*. Note: microfibre is also used for mop heads and dusters, among other things. Note also: some E-Cloths are now impregnated with particles of silver, which has powerful antibacterial properties.

paper towels

According to Friends of the Earth, paper accounts for one quarter of household waste. And the World Wildlife Federation says that EU production of paper consumables destroys 25 million trees a year. You can cut some of that waste with little effort and no sacrifice.

Now, some advocates of green living say that you shouldn't use paper towels in the first place. I do not support that view: the towels are just too useful, and outright opposition is pointless because so many people are going to go on using them whatever any eco-

warrior says. But if you choose to use paper towels, you should use them sensibly.

Here is how not to use them: use three squares to wipe a drop of milk from a toddler's chin, then throw away; to wipe a table clean, then throw away; throw a few squares on a floor that's received a splash of water, then throw away. That kind of thoughtless profligacy turns green cooks red with rage.

So, how to use them? There are three principles for green cooks:
• Use towels made from recycled paper or sustainably managed trees.
• Use washable cloths as much as possible. Whenever you reach for a paper towel, ask yourself, 'Could I be using something non-disposable?'
• Get the most out of paper towels. Use one square, not two or three. And drop the idea that it must always be thrown away after one use. Unless you've applied it to something noxious, stash it in a jar under the sink and deploy it in any activity where food-safe cleanliness is not required. Examples: mopping a small food-spill from the floor, wiping the hob, wiping food-smeared plates. If you compost, the finally-exhausted paper can go into it. But don't recycle them; they're classified as 'contaminated' waste.

rags

Someone in your household is going to hate me for saying this. If there are teenaged children around, they may die of embarrassment. But I have to say it anyway. In the Green Kitchen, you should be turning old clothes into rags.

This statement does not refer to clothing that's in good enough condition to be given to charity. It refers to terminally tattered T-shirts, jeans with more holes than a spider's web and the like. All can be reused for lengthy periods before they eventually bite the dust. Some tips:

• Cut up large items. The back of a shirt can used for straining stock or even preserves, though the sleeves must content themselves with cleaning work.

• Cotton/polyester shirts: can also be used in place of paper towels.

• Denim: use for heavy jobs, such as mopping the kitchen floor or a crusty hob.

• Old bath towels: cut them up and turn into all-purpose kitchen wipes.

• Wash every garment before it migrates from wardrobe to kitchen. To make doubly sure it's food-safe, you can take it straight from washing machine to microwave. A wet cotton cloth takes 3 minutes to sterilise in the microwave. Smaller items need less, though a little more time won't hurt. But do make sure the items are wet before microwaving.

• If the rags will come into contact with food, make sure they're colourfast.

It takes some courage to go from riches to rags. My own wife, though very green-minded, draws the line at squares made from old jeans. The children ask that rags be stored out of sight when guests are coming to the house. I don't blame them, either.

8.
reducing waste

According to Friends of the Earth, everyone in England and Wales throws away rubbish weighing 7 times his or her body-weight per annum. The kitchen accounts for around 20 per cent of that figure. With little effort, you can cut your contribution to the rubbish-mountain by as much as 75 per cent.

packaging

Needless to say, the fight against kitchen waste begins when you buy your food. If you buy it in some kind of packaging, this needs to be disposed of when the food has been used. And over-packaged food is a waste of resources, using energy and raw materials (some from fossil fuels) at every stage from manufacture onwards.

Having said that, I must add immediately that it's possible to lose perspective on this subject. By weight, all packaging (including food) accounts for a tiny fraction, perhaps 1 per cent, of total waste. And manufacturers and retailers – who pay for the packaging, remember – have made a lot of progress in cutting it down to a minimum. Moreover, the really outrageous waste in packaging tends to occur in non-food merchandise. If you have ever bought a memory card for a camera or computer (weighing 1g) in a 150g plastic sleeve, you know what I mean.

Some packaging, such as the glass in a bottle or the metal in a tin of beans, can't be avoided and is economic to recycle. Some is avoidable, and that's what you need to watch for. Some tips:

• Buy loose fruit and vegetables rather than pre-selected packs in film-wrapped trays. There are reusable produce bags that you can carry with you on shopping trips, and you should look out for them.

• Don't put fresh produce in the retailer's plastic bags if you can avoid it. A bunch of bananas, a butternut squash, a single baking potato – these things do not need to be bagged.

• If you do get plastic bags, save them and take them out with you on future shopping trips. They can be used repeatedly unless they're dirty.

• Reuse clean bags for food storage – they are food-safe.

• If you buy fruit or vegetables in a film-wrapped package, unwrap the film carefully. You may be able to reuse it.

• A final word in unfashionable praise of packaging. Some of what *seems* unnecessary – the plastic wrapping on a cucumber, or the film-wrapped tray of apples – may actually cut greenhouse gas emissions by reducing food waste. See more on the next page.

food waste

One of the major areas for waste reduction lies in cutting down the amount of food you throw away. Total food waste accounts for around one third of household waste. And in the UK, as of the year 2007, we threw away around a third of the food we bought every year, usually in methane-emitting landfill. It weighed 6.7 million tonnes. It cost £9 billion. Eliminating the waste would be the equivalent of taking 1 in 5 cars off the road.

How can you avoid adding to that mountain of wasted food? Here are a few pointers:

• Shop daily, and ideally for no more than 2 days of eating, so you can keep a close watch on what you buy.

• Make a detailed list based on the upcoming week's meals if you have to do a large weekly shopping trip. And stick to it.

• Check your fridge and larder before you go on a shopping trip. This isn't in order to find out what you need; it's to find out what you don't need. Some people have an irresistible need to buy certain foods – my personal weakness is lemons –

whenever they go shopping. The sight of a dozen unopened lemons will act as a deterrent.

• Don't be tempted by special offers on food you don't have a plan for; they're not cheap if you're not going to use them. And try to buy fresh produce in places that allow you to choose exactly the number and quantity that you want. If you need just two potatoes, but you have to buy a big bag of them, the surplus is almost certain to get thrown away.

• Try to shop in small food shops, if it's at all possible. Supermarkets are designed to encourage excessive purchasing.

• Do your best to avoid temptation. As Hannibal Lecter says in a somewhat different context: 'How do we begin to covet...? We begin by coveting what we see....' In a supermarket, you see everything. It all looks so enticing, and you think to yourself, 'maybe I'll treat myself just this once'. Don't! Today's coveted treat is tomorrow's invisible package at the back of the fridge and next week's passenger on a long trip to the landfill site. Take that list with you, and stick to it.

bottled and filtered water

Most people don't need a water filter any more than they need bottled water. The standards of purity for tap water are very high, and I'll bet that in a blind tasting you couldn't tell your tap water from something that had gone through a filter. I've done this with friends who use a water filter, and in every case they preferred the unfiltered water. Filtering your water is not a grave insult to the environment, apart from the disposal of the used filters, but it's not something you need to do.

Bottled water, by contrast, is a very serious environmental problem. Our foolish addiction to the stuff uses large quantities of energy. The bottles, whether glass or plastic, have to be manufactured – using non-renewable fossil fuels. More energy is used (along with other resources) to bottle, package, store and ship it. Getting the stuff from shop to home adds further to the CO2 emissions; the bulk and weight of water in bottles means that a shopping trip that might otherwise be carried out by foot or bicycle necessitates the use of a car, however close the shop. And all this

for a product that is no safer or tastier than the water that flows, at 1/1000 the price, out of our taps. The writer Ian Williams, in the excellent *What to Eat* by Professor Marion Nestle, describes bottled water as 'ostentatiously useless'.

If you are addicted to bottled water, I beg you to conduct the following experiment. Take two bottles, one empty and one containing your store-bought water. Fill the empty one with tap water, then refrigerate both overnight. Overnight chilling brings them to identical temperatures and allows any odour of chlorine (a harmless and essential anti-microbial) to dissipate.

In the morning, get someone to pour the waters into two glasses without telling you which is which. Taste them side by side. Can you identify them? If your blind tasting reveals no difference, quit your expensive, environmentally destructive habit on the spot.

carrier bags

In my column in *The Times,* no subject arouses more passion among readers than the pros and cons of plastic carrier bags. Some people hate them, as I do; some defend them; some point out that their contribution to landfill is minimal by comparison with other household waste. There's a bit of truth in all the opposing views on this complex and contentious subject.

But I stick to my basic opposition, despite the complexities. The production of plastic carrier bags uses millions of litres of oil every year. In landfill, they persist for over 100 years. Improperly disposed of in both land-based and marine environments, they damage the natural scene and can kill birds and fish. Banning them seems like the good option to me.

Opponents of a carrier-bag ban say that they don't just throw them away but reuse them as rubbish bags. If they didn't get free carrier bags, they would have to buy plastic bin liners which are larger and often thicker than carrier bags. (And by the way, all retailers have made great progress in reducing the amount of plastic used in their bags.)

I respect their arguments, but I have done home experiments to compare the rubbish-storage capacity of carrier bags and bin liners. The heaviest bin liner weighed six times more than the lightest carrier bag. I then filled a carrier bag with as much household rubbish as it would accommodate, which wasn't much, and transferred the rubbish to a large bin liner. Without testing scientifically (not enough rubbish!), I estimated that I could get at least ten times more stuff into the bin

liners than into the carrier bags. Even using the lightest carrier bag and the heaviest bin liner for comparison, the calculations are easy. You throw away less plastic when you use proper bin liners.

Retailers hand bags out for free, but they're not free. We pay for them in an extra slice of profit for the retailer – around 18 billion bags every year in the UK. If we crave the luxury of carrying our groceries in instantly discarded, highly polluting receptacles made from fossil fuels, we should pay for it. If recycling becomes universal, I will change my tune. In the meantime, it's uneconomic. Burning them may be the better solution.

Numerous towns, cities and whole countries have banned the distribution of plastic bags. In Ireland they've been charging shoppers for bags since 2002 and this has reduced bag handouts by 90 per cent. Expect to see more of these initiatives in years to come, especially if the price of oil stays high.

There are alternatives to ordinary carrier bags. One is the 'degradable' plastic bag, incorporating an additive that makes it break down more quickly. But the additive mustn't get into recycled plastic, and degradable bags don't break down so quickly in anaerobic landfill. Another is biodegradable bags made from starch and vegetable oil. But these produce methane in landfill, and methane is a potent greenhouse gas. These bags have to be composted.

The best alternative is still a product that can be reused indefinitely: a bag made of fabric such as jute or cotton, durable plastic such as polypropylene, or a combination of materials. Supermarkets are increasingly offering these as an alternative to disposable bags, selling them at low cost. The best are those with a flat rectangular base and four walls that sit up straight when the bag is empty. They can hold five or six times more shopping than a disposable bag, and because the handles are wide and sturdy, they don't cut into your hands even when the bag is heavy with shopping.

The other alternative, ideal for those who do their grocery shopping by car, is a collapsible box – or a few of them, if you do a large weekly shop. These may be made of plastic or of fabric on a plastic frame. They fold up neatly when empty, so you can carry them in your supermarket trolley without using up a lot of space. When you get to the checkout, just unfold the box and put your shopping in it. The boxes are then unloaded into your car and carried into the house. Unload them and fold them up again for neat home storage.

composting

If you have a garden, even just some house plants, you owe it to the planet to compost as much food waste as possible. On top of the 6.7 million tonnes of wasted food thrown away every year, there's the legitimate food waste: apple cores, eggshells and so on. You can either pack this a plastic bag and send it to a landfill site, producing methane (after the bag's broken up, in a century or more); or put it in a sealed container in your garden, where worms will gradually eat and digest it, breaking it down into organic matter to become part of the earth again.

Before I started composting, I threw away, on average, three large plastic bags of kitchen waste every week. This was for a family of five. When I started composting, that figure went down to one bag a week. When we got a 'hot' composter (see opposite), it went down to between zero and one bag a week.

Composting is a simple process, though you have to learn a few simple rules and then pay a bit of attention. The work involved takes around 20 minutes spread over a week and there are several options. The one you choose will depend on the size of your garden and household, and your meat consumption. The descriptions that follow are brief, because composting is a gardening issue and there is so much good advice available from other sources.

Basic composting requires a large container, usually barrel-shaped or resembling a cone with the tip cut off. The bottom of the composter is open, so it is fully exposed to the ground underneath, and it should have an opening near the base for easy extraction of finished compost.

The composter should be placed in a spot that gets some sun; heat helps your food waste break down faster. You can further accelerate breakdown by using special commercial treatments, available in garden centres, and this might be a good idea if you have a large family but a limited amount of space for the composter itself. The biggest trick to composting is getting the right balance of waste material. The two compostable categories are 'green' and 'brown'.
• Green means kitchen waste such as vegetables, fruit, teabags or tea leaves. Citrus waste can be included, but it takes longer to

break down than other fruits so chop it into smallish pieces before composting. Green waste can also come from the garden, in the form of grass cuttings and prunings.

- Brown waste is generally dry material from non-food sources: egg boxes, cardboard or paper, and autumn leaves.
- Other compostables include eggshells (crushed and added with brown waste) and ashes (from wood only) from the fireplace.
- Definitely to be excluded from the ordinary composter: meat, cooked food, animal waste.
- Cut large items of kitchen waste into smaller pieces, so the compost will be more compact. This is especially important if you find the bin is filling up too quickly.

wormeries

These can be kept indoors in some circumstances, and they produce usable compost more quickly than ordinary composters. Wormeries are usually sold in the form of a container incorporating three or more trays with perforated bases. The worms in the first tray are fed your kitchen waste, and when that fills up you put the second tray on top and use that. By the time the third tray is full, the bottom tray should have usable compost and can be emptied into a separate container or used in the garden.

'hot' composters

These omnivorous, sealed containers are secure from garden pests. That means they can take meat, bones, fish and cooked food waste – which makes them the number-one choice if you (a) eat meat and (b) have a large enough garden to accommodate their substantial size. (Though they are no larger than many ordinary composters.) Hot composters may cost around 50 per cent more than ordinary composters, but in meat- and fish-eating households, they cut the volume of landfill-production dramatically. They generate high heat because of their design, so they don't need to be in a sunny spot. They need to be fed the right stuff, around two parts green to one part brown. Having used one for several years, I can promise that this is no big deal. The ideal choice for maximum reduction of food waste.

the bokashi

The Bokashi uses bran mixed with yeast, bacteria and fungi to digest food waste. You put the waste in a plastic tub, sprinkle on the bran and close the lid. As more waste gets produced, add it with another layer of bran. When the bin is full, leave it for a couple of weeks to let the micro-organisms ferment the scraps until they form a compact mass that can be dug into soil or added to your compost bin. Bokashis are usually sold in pairs: while the first one is fermenting, you use the second. Bokashi waste can be chucked with your household rubbish. It fills less space and breaks down more quickly. But I'd suggest giving it to a grateful gardener. A Bokashi is best for small households that don't produce much waste – unless it's used together with an ordinary composter, whose work it will accelerate.

index

aluminium foil 27
appliances 20
asparagus
  lidded asparagus 54
  maccheroncini alla Saffi 62
aubergines, summery 77

bacon 38, 104, 107
beans 174
  basic braised beans 119, 174
  beans and a bone 125
  lid-fried green beans 48
  spicy bean patties 176
  Tuscan-style bean soup 175
béchamel 161, 162, 163
beef
  beef steaks 39
  beef stew with chickpeas and lemon 130
  curried beef 129
  shin of beef with Chinese-style sauce 181
  short ribs with beer and spices 128
  sliced beef casserole 94
blenders 21
Bokashis 205
bottled water 201
broccoli with oyster sauce 75
Brussels sprouts with shallots 117
bulk preparation 178
butternut squash 121
butternut and carrot soup 106
butternut squash with béchamel 163

cabbage
  braised cabbage 114
  braised red cabbage 115
  cabbage soup with bacon 104
  cabbage with caraway 53
  cabbage with vinegar and garlic 144
  quickest lid-braised cabbage 54
carbonara 80
carrier bags 202–203
carrot and butternut soup 106
carrots glazed with honey 57
cauliflower and leek soup 104
celery
  creamed celery with red peppers 56
  lid-steamed celery 49
  squid and celery 'stir-fry' 86
chicken 172, 178
  chicken congee 133
  chicken curry for one 89
  chicken in a pot with saffron cream 90
  chicken pieces under the lid 36
  chicken soup with new season's garlic 108
  chicken with forty cloves of garlic 137
  chicken with limes and spicy tomato sauce 120
  chicken, barley and bacon soup 107
  chicken, squash, turnips and spices 121

red-cooked chicken 37
  roasted chicken pieces with lemon and cumin 184
  Thai curry, red or green 122
chicory, micro-braised 76
chilli sauce, Singaporean 47
chilli, tomato and garlic relish 46
chorizo, instant 97
cleaning 186
clingfilm 27
composting 204–205
courgette salad with prosciutto 142
courgette soup with lemongrass 104
courgettes and tomatoes 52
courgettes, creamed 69

defrosting food 91
dishwashers 9
double-dipping sauce 47

equipment 8

fennel 173
  fennel and new potatoes with rosemary and garlic 184
  fennel salad with mustard vinaigrette 140
filtered water 201
fish 172
  lidded fish en papillote 33
  quick fish curry 84
  salted and marinated fish 146
  simple salmon 82
  variations for steamed fish 83
flooring 16–17
food processors 23

food storage 25, 150
food waste 200
freezers 10–11
freezing 151, 172, 178
fridges 10–11

garlic 108, 120, 137
  garlic and mushroom sauce 79
  garlic mushrooms 73
  tomato, garlic and chilli relish 46
ginger sauce, Cantonese 47
grills 160
guinea fowl with cider and spices 124
gurnard in tomato sauce 87

Hannibal Lecter 200
hamburgers 40
hearty vegetable soup 105
herbed béchamel 162
hobs 14–15
hot composters 205

juicers 23

kettles 22

lamb
  lamb fillet 43
  lamb loin chops 39
  lamb shanks with apricots 126
leek and cauliflower soup 104
leek and potato soup 103
lemon 97, 130, 184
lentils, simple 172
lentils with fennel and red peppers 173
lettuce, quick-braised 50
lidded cookery 28–29, 30–31, 48, 49, 51

lighting 18
mackerel ceviche 146
marinade for salted fish 147
meat 31, 92–93, 172, 180
spicy meat loaf with Thai flavours 95
microfibre cloths 195
microwaves 20–21, 64–65
cooking vessels 66
defrosting food 91
meat 92–93
timing 67
vegetables 68–69
mornay sauce 162
multiple cooking 148–150, 180
preparation 178
single ingredients 152
mushrooms 79
garlic mushrooms 73
pure mushrooms 96
stuffed mushrooms 55
mustard sauce 162

no-cook cooking 138

okra, Barbara Kafka's stewed 75
onions
fried onions 44
sage and onion sauce 78
sauce soubise 166
soffrito 167
oven cooking 158–159
dual cooking 179
ingredients temperatures 158
whole meals 182–183
ovens 12–13

packaging 199
pans 24
frying pans 32
panzanella 141
paper towels 196

parsnip gratin 164
pasta 31
peach cobbler, southern-style 185
peas with mint and lime 73
peppers
creamed celery with red peppers 56
grilled peppers in the microwave and a frying pan 70
lentils with fennel and red peppers 173
peppers and basil 61
roasted peppers with anchovies and capers 183
pheasant with bacon, port and grapes 38
piggybacking 158
plastic bottles 209
plastic boxes 25
pork
casserole of belly pork 180
pork congee 133
pork loin chops 43
pork, potatoes and crackling 127
rustic terrine 135
potatoes
baked potatoes 69
crushed hash browns 155
dinner-party potatoes 155
fennel and new potatoes with rosemary and garlic 184
instant gratin 155
leek and potato soup 103
lidded new potatoes 59, 154
new potatoes in white sauce 164
pork, potatoes and crackling 127
potato and rocket soup 106
potato salad 154

potatoes for mashing 58
pressure cooking 112
roast potatoes in a pan 58
pots 24
poultry 31, 88, 92
prawns, gambas al ajillo 85
pressure cooking 98–101
double-cooked dishes 136
potatoes 113
potted dishes 134
rice 132
soup 102
vegetables 110–111
PTFE sheets 26
pulses 31, 118, 172

rags 197
reducing waste 198
residual heat 29
rice
basic risotto 132
congee 133
fried rice 157
leftover soup 156
quicker congee 156
rice pudding 157
soupy rice 157
rocket and potato soup 106

sage and onion sauce 78
salmon
cured salmon 145
salmon, lemon, dill 97
salmon steak au poivre 34
salsa verde 45
sausage and tomatoes 60
sausages, lidded 42
seasonal gluts 168
serial meals 51
serving dishes 187
sinks 193
soffrito 167
soup 102, 105
soup base 171
sour cream sauce 47

spaghetti all'aglio, olio e peperoncini 80
squid and celery 'stir-fry' 86
stock 171
sweet potatoes, my mother's 74
sweetcorn from heaven 70

tomatoes 87
cherry tomatoes 96
courgettes and tomatoes 52
sausage and tomatoes 60
simple tomato sauce 168
spicy gazpacho with sherry vinegar 139
spicy stuffed tomato 142
tomato sauce with pancetta 79
tomato, garlic and chilli relish 46
tomatoes with balsamic vinaigrette and fresh herbs 76

vegetables 31
creamy vegetables 163
hearty vegetable soup 105
lidded frying 48
microwaves 68–69
pressure cooking 110–111
steamed vegetable dishes 113
vegetarian congee 133
velouté sauce 162

washing up 188
brushes 191
reusing pots and pans 189
soaking 190–191
stacking 190
worktops 19
wormeries 205

yogurt and dill relish 46

Useful web addresses

www.est.org.uk
The Energy Saving Trust

www.waterwise.org.uk
Information and guidance on
reducing water consumption

http://tiny.cc/s9NoD
Source for experiment on heating
water by different methods

www.missvickie.com
Information and recipes for
pressure cookers

www.microwaveassociation.org.uk
Technical info and recipes

www.eartheasy.com
A useful resource for cleaning

www.foe.co.uk
Friends of the Earth

www.recycle-more.co.uk
Recycling information

www.howtocompost.org/
An American composting site

http://www.green-pan.com/
Green Pan

www.lakeland.co.uk
Lakeland

www.falconproducts.co.uk
Falcon Products

www.smartmicrofibre.co.uk
Microfibre Cleaning Solutions

www.e-cloth.com
E-Cloths – top microfibre brand

www.greengardener.co.uk
Gardening supplies, composters,
Bokashis

Books Cited in the Text

Special thanks to Barbara Kafka,
who has taught me nearly
everything I know about
microwave cooking.

Julia Child *The French Chef
Cookbook* (Alfred A Knopf,
1968)
Craig Claiborne & Virginia Lee
The Chinese Cookbook (André
Deutsch, 1973)
*Good Housekeeping Microwave
Handbook* (Ebury 1986)
Marcella Hazan *Classic Italian
Cookbook* (Alfred A Knopf,
1976)
*Second Italian Classic
Cookbook* (Macmillan, 1990)
Fergus Henderson *Nose to Tail
Cooking* (Bloomsbury, 2004)
Barbara Kafka *Microwave
Gourmet* (William Morrow,
1987)
Nico Ladenis & Alan Crompton-
Batt *My Gastronomy* (Ebury
Press, 1987)
Tess Mallos *The Complete
Middle East Cookbook*
(Grub Street, 2004)
Marion Nestle *What to Eat*
(North Point Press, 2006)
Julie Sahni *Classic Indian
Vegetarian Cooking* (Grub
Street, 2003)
Kelly Simon *Thai Cooking* (Little
Brown, 1993)
Yan-Kit So *Classic Food of
China* (Macmillan, 1992)
Robert L. Wolke *What Einstein
Told His Cook* (W W Norton,
2002)

Acknowledgements

My first thanks go to *The Times*
for commissioning the weekly
column. Special thanks to my
sceptically sharp-eyed editor,
Tony Turnbull. No journalist
could ask for a better editor.

Second thanks to my editors at
Kyle Cathie: Caroline Taggart
and Jenny Wheatley, and copy-
editor Sally Somers.

Third thanks: to my agents
Michael Alcock and Anna Powe
of Johnson & Alcock. They
pushed me to write this book
when my natural sloth would
have kept it simmering (with a
lid on, of course) for years.

Miscellaneous thanks to:
everyone at B&M Seafoods;
John Bullock; Emma Marsden;
Aggie Mackenzie; Nigel Slater;
John Whiting; the Guild of Foo
Writers; Russell Morgan; and
Tefal, for giving me a pressure
cooker. For reasons they alone
will understand fully, I extend
special thoughts of goodwill to
Mark and Clare Dally.

Fourth and utterly inadequate
thanks to my wife, Emma Dally.

And finally: thanks to my
mother, Norma Solway Ehrlich,
who taught me the virtues of
careful resource-management,
and to my late father, Eugene
Ehrlich, who died as this book
was nearing completion. Had I
not inherited his love of precisio
in language, I might be practisin
resource-management in private